The ~~Hippocratic~~ Hypocritical Oath

One physicians willingness to fight for America's health.

By Daniel Thompson, M.D.

Published by Daniel Thompson, M.D.
4856 Sawmill Rd. PMB# 307
Columbus, Ohio 43235

Copyright © 1999 by Daniel Thompson, M.D.

All rights reserved. No part of this book may be reproduced or transmitted in any form or by any means, electronic or mechanical, including photocopying, recording, or by any information storage and retrieval system, without permission in writing from the author.

Printed in Canada
1st printing 1999
ISBN: 0-9677872-0-3

Cover and book design by Jill Dible

Table of Contents

Preface 5

Introduction: The Raid 11

PART 1: Obesity 19

PART 2: Internet Medicine 45

PART 3: Skeletons, Personal Views & Updates 87

Epilogue 139

Appendix A: Ohio Weight Loss Rules 141

Appendix B: Cyber Doc 153

Appendix C: References 169

Appendix D: New Ohio Internet Regulations 173

Preface

All physicians who receive their medical degrees in this country are supposed to uphold certain standards with regards to medical ethics. These standards have not changed for over 1,000 years since they were first written down by a Greek physician named Hippocrates. I took the Hippocratic oath in 1983 when I graduated from Medical school, and since that time I have come to believe that this oath is being threatened by the very agencies that are supposed to help physicians protect that oath.

I also believe that many physicians have not been living by this Hippocratic oath, but rather by what I call the hypocritical oath. A hypocrite is someone who does not live up to the moral standards he or she expects others to live by. For instance, a physician who refuses to treat a patient with a known disease and then persecutes a colleague for treating that patient is a hypocrite. In Ohio and many other states, physicians refuse to treat the disease known as obesity and then persecute those physicians who are willing to treat this deadly disease. Secondly, many physicians treat patients by calling in prescriptions without ever seeing the patient in person or actually examining them. Pharmacy boards allow this practice and physicians depend on this freedom when they get calls from patients at night, on weekends, and when taking call for other physicians. Yet, these same physicians and pharmacy boards would like to make it illegal for doctors to prescribe medications for patients via the Internet because those doctors don't see their Internet patients in person. That is hypocrisy.

The Hippocratic oath states:

I solemnly pledge myself to consecrate my life to the service of humanity.

I will give my teachers the respect and gratitude, which is their due.

I will practice my profession with conscience and dignity.

The health of my patient will be my first consideration.

I will respect the secrets which are confided in me, even after the patient has died.

I will maintain by all means in my power, the honor and the noble traditions of the medical profession.

My colleagues will be my brothers.

I will not permit considerations of religion, nationality, race, party politics, or social standing to intervene between my duty and my patient.

I will maintain the utmost respect for human life from the time of conception; even under threat I will not use my medical knowledge contrary to the laws of humanity.

I make these promises solemnly, freely, and upon my honor.

My name is Daniel Thompson and I have been a physician in Ohio for over 15 years. When I began writing this book, I was under investigation for drug trafficking, racketeering, and money laundering by several Ohio agencies. Prior to finishing this book, I was indicted and charged with 64 counts of either selling or trafficking dangerous drugs. I hope that after reading this book you will agree that these charges are an unjust attempt to punish one physician for

PREFACE

practices, which all physicians perform and consider standard methods of practicing traditional medicine.

I had several reasons for writing this book. First, I hope to change American perceptions about a serious disease called obesity. It is my contention that American physicians have allowed millions of people with this disease to go untreated. This is an ugly travesty and a national shame. According to former Surgeon General C. Everett Koop, 300,000 Americans die every year because of obesity. Several hundred thousand more develop other serious diseases every year because their obesity was never treated. My second goal is to defend Internet medicine against attacks by the medical establishment. I hope to show that Internet medicine is inevitable and that the agencies attempting to ban it prefer to protect traditional medical practices rather than to improve medical care for all Americans. Finally, this book represents part of my defense against allegations that have been made against me by some very powerful institutions. The following pages will reveal that I am an aggressive and caring physician who is willing to fight for better health care in this country.

Medical care has changed drastically over the twentieth century. Physicians today, for example, rarely make house calls; in fact, patients often have to wait weeks to be seen by a physician. Doctors have become the gatekeepers for America's health care. Physicians decide what medication you can have, what hospital you can be admitted to, and when you can see them. Most Americans do not get to choose which physician they see for their medical care. That physician is decided upon by the insurance company or HMO; that is, if the patient is lucky enough to have insurance. Even the HMO or insurer is often determined by the individual's employer. It has almost gotten to the point where patients have no say in what doctor they get to see.

However, some Americans are just now starting to experience a new way of obtaining their health care, one that is actually convenient—and they like it! This new and better way is called Internet medicine; a development which I believe will revolutionize the way medicine is practiced in this country.

As a physician working toward this revolution, I am now at risk of going to jail—primarily for helping to heal people who have a disease that is common, treatable, and causes more deaths in this country every year than most Americans could even imagine. That disease is called obesity. Millions of Americans desperately want to lose weight and cannot do so without medical treatment. No one should suffer discrimination in this country because they have a disease. And no one should be refused treatment.

Not many physicians have hands-on experience in both of my specialties: obesity and Internet medicine. Unfortunately, however, many of the opponents of obesity medication and Internet medicine who cannot say they have any expertise with either issue, still criticize them.

Until now, the most difficult endeavor I've ever accomplished was becoming a physician. However, writing this book has proven a close second! I never realized how difficult it is to sit down and write something and then organize it well enough for others to make cohesive sense of it. I have attempted to keep this book simple so that it is not so technical as to lose its emotion. My goal is for you to be able to read this book and receive its contents in the same way that

PREFACE

you would listen to a family member tell you their version of a story.

To some readers, my story may appear biased or one-sided, but I would ask those readers to bear with me and also to ask themselves whether they have been subjected to less-recognizable biases before. Obesity is portrayed negatively and unfairly in most magazines, newspapers, and on television, and many people still think weight-loss medications are dangerous and/or addictive. Also, many readers have probably never heard anything positive about Internet medicine. A current trend among the media favors attacking "the dangers of Internet medicine" in this country. Considering how much my patients love Internet medical services, it is odd that most of the media coverage of this subject has been rather negative.

Remember Star Trek and the little black box that was used by the doctor? In many ways, that little black box already exists! Technology will soon replace some, but not all, physicians. It seems ironic that I worked so hard to become a good physician to end up fighting for the technology that may soon replace me.

I hope to change the way you think about doctors, medicine, and your rights to certain medical treatment. I want to empower you by illustrating, with examples, some of the existing flaws in our medical system and how *unimportant* your personal physician is to your general health and well being! I want to also change your position on how you feel about the 60+% of our overweight society, whether you are in that percentage or not. I will illustrate how much power pharmaceutical companies, state pharmacy, and state medical boards have in the U.S. Finally; I will show you how much more power you have compared to these companies and agencies.

You live in a unique time. You can have a part in changing health care and making the simple forms of treatment more readily available to those wanting and needing such treatment. I feel it is very rare for a person to have the chance to make a stand for something he or she believes in—something significant, decent, and morally correct. Unfortunately, when one man stands alone, he loses! A smart man enlists the help of a force that is greater than that of his adversary. I am one man looking for recruits. I am the underdog and I represent something good for the average patient.

I cannot win the battle for obesity and Internet medicine against these powerful forces by myself. However, with the help of some of you, I cannot lose.

Introduction: The Raid

On the 17th of February, 1999, my company had some unexpected visitors. My partner and I were sitting in our office working when ten unmarked cars sped into our corporate parking lot, disgorging police officers who soon surrounded our place of business.

We opened our doors and were immediately handed a search warrant. The judge who had approved the warrant believed the State Pharmacy Board's claim that we were drug trafficking, racketeering, and money laundering.

This is what I would consider a bad day at work!

The police officers just happened to have our pharmacy application with them during the raid. The officer who handed it back to us told us they had decided to inform us that we would not be approved for such a license, and that they had delivered the application personally since they were coming anyway!

The Columbus, Ohio, narcotics squad, in conjunction with the State Pharmacy Board, interviewed all of our employees; then, they had me walk them through our Internet medicine business operations. From our office they removed completed, processed orders already packaged in UPS envelopes. They took all of our patient files, our computers, disks, ledgers, receipts, and more.

Finally, they informed us that we were not being charged with anything.

They concluded this extremely invasive raid by explaining that they planned on presenting all the evidence from this search to a Grand Jury with the aim of getting an indictment against us as soon as possible. We were told that we could be handcuffed, and that if the police officers wanted they could take us downtown for further questioning. And yet they also said that we were not being ordered to stop doing Internet medicine per se—we were told simply that doing Internet medicine was wrong and that we ought to feel morally compelled to stop doing it.

As you will see in the following chapters, my office did not start practicing Internet medicine until our attorneys had researched it and verified that it was not illegal. But even our attorneys—competent attorneys who represent one of the most reputable law firms in Ohio—never predicted that an Internet medicine practitioner could be accused of drug trafficking.

I began to practice Internet medicine only after being reassured that in the worst-case scenario I would at least receive a phone call or letter from the State Pharmacy Board before being asked to stop doing Internet medicine in some states. According to the research we did before beginning to offer medicine over the Internet, not one other physician practicing Internet medicine in this country has been abused like I eventually was by such agencies. Nobody expected how ruthless the Ohio State Pharmacy Board would be. I never thought I would have to call my Dad and let him know I might be going to prison for practicing medicine on the Internet.

Several days after the raid our bank accounts were frozen. My name and photos of me were immediately broadcast on all local television networks so that everyone could learn about the Internet physician charged with drug trafficking. Under current drug enforcement laws, governmental agencies are allowed to seize all of a suspect's assets after being granted a search warrant for money laundering, racketeering, and drug trafficking. No trial is necessary to determine if you are guilty or innocent. In less than one week, my entire career was annihilated without me even being charged with doing anything wrong.

But the issue the police, the State Pharmacy Board, and the media all focus on which is the most hypocritical of all—the basis for their horrible accusation of drug trafficking—was that I was treating patients with drugs without actually seeing or examining these patients.

This book will help to show why this claim represents a tragic misunderstanding of how Internet medicine works. Not only that, it shows a total lack of awareness of how traditional, face-to-face medicine works—or fails to.

Thus, on February 17th I went from being a well-respected Ohio physician to being an alleged drug trafficker, racketeer, and money launderer. When my partner and I met with several criminal attorneys, we were told that these serious accusations enabled the government to seize all of our assets without even getting an indictment against us. Fighting these agencies would be expensive. Without money, we would lose and face prison sentences. Every attorney we talked with admitted that we would not stand a chance of winning a trial if we had to use a public defender.

Of course, my immediate reaction to all of this was to question why it was happening. What did I do that made these agencies so angry? Was it my weight-loss practice, and really not about Internet medicine? Was it Internet medicine, and not really about weight loss? Perhaps I became an immediate threat to somebody who decided to squash me?

Yes. I have concluded that my medical practice is a major threat to Ohio's State Pharmacy and Medical Boards. The truth is that I am threatening the state of Ohio's weight-loss rules. Not only that, Internet medicine poses another threat. There is no other explanation as to why I was never notified by these agencies that they would like me to stop my Internet practice until they could evaluate it. A phone call or a letter would have been sufficient—not a search warrant with accusations they knew would destroy my career! Not seizing our equipment and breaking a trust I have with my Internet patients by calling them and destroying their patient-doctor confidentiality. Not by freezing our company assets.

Obviously, these agencies have power to do almost whatever they want! I cannot believe anyone would accept that the treatment of baldness, herpes, sexual dysfunction, nicotine addiction, and obesity over the Internet by a Board-Certified Internal Medicine physician is drug trafficking. Certainly, a physician who merely treats his patients with approved medications for approved diseases does not deserve such threats. I can only assume that the agencies that sought to prosecute me perceived in me a threat—not that they were concerned for the safety of my Internet patients.

The story eventually became clear: two brothers from Ohio, with Ohio addresses, applied for weight-loss medicines and my office agreed (against its standard procedure) to supply them. These two brothers, it turned out, worked for the State Pharmacy Board. But that is getting ahead of my story.

INTRODUCTION

The crux of the matter is this: I believe that I have been a good physician. I hope that after reading this book you will agree that this prosecution of me is malicious and misguided. I am not a drug trafficker and I hope to convince you of why I feel able to say this with 100 percent certainty. Before I can do so I feel obligated to explain why I became a bariatrician—a physician who treats obesity.

In 1983, after receiving my MD from the Ohio State College of Medicine, I did a three-year Internal Medicine residency at Mt. Carmel Medical Center, also located in Columbus. There, I was chief resident during my third year of residency. I became board certified in Internal Medicine in 1988. I remained in Columbus and practiced medicine as an emergency room trauma physician from 1986 to 1996, a total of 13 years.

In 1996, I left the fast-paced emergency room practice to start a private practice where I specifically treated overweight patients. Unfortunately, in doing so, I lost the respect of some of my fellow physicians. For some reason, bariatrics is just not regarded very highly in Ohio. Many of my colleagues were astounded that anyone could quit being a trauma physician in order to take care of obese patients. They did not feel I was taking on a legitimate medical practice. I was even called a quack by some doctors. I found myself surrounded by physicians who did not believe obesity was even a disease at all. Physicians like to describe those patients afflicted with obesity as being *fat*. They are not *fat*—medically they should be described as overweight, obese, or morbidly obese.

I started seeing patients in May of 1996 and by July of

that same year I had two weight-loss centers in Columbus. I was seeing almost 200 patients every day—that is no exaggeration! I was definitely correct about the lack of competition. I personally treated over 4,000 clients in a two-year period—more people afflicted with obesity than most physicians will treat in their lifetime! I would venture to say that I am an expert bariatrician in Ohio, simply because there are not many physicians in Ohio who are willing to treat their obese patients.

At the time I started my weight-loss clinic, the medicine Phen-Fen was being used to treat obesity throughout this country and I decided to use it on my patients. Many physicians did not feel that I was making a rational decision, even though the medications were FDA-approved. Phen-Fen consisted of two individual weight-loss medications called Phentermine and Fenfluramine. Both of these medications were FDA-approved for weight loss individually, but had been used in combination with increasing frequency by physicians for almost 10 years in this country. Because of my decision to treat obese patients with weight-loss medication, I was ostracized from the medical community. Some of them thought I was going to treat my patients with amphetamines. And many of them felt that medications would not work because patients would gain back their weight as soon as they stopped taking their medication. It was amazing to me how little my fellow physicians really knew about the treatment of obesity.

I used Phen-Fen in my weight-loss centers until it was voluntarily taken off of the market because of negative media coverage that reported heart valve problems stemming from use of the medication. However, I still believe that the Phen-Fen combination was nothing short of miraculous for the treatment of obesity in the patients under my care. With Phen-Fen off the market, my centers remained open and I continued to administer other weight-loss medications, including Meridia™ and Phentermine. My success in treating obesity continued, although not having Phen-Fen to use as a weapon in the fight was a setback.

The more criticism I heard from my colleagues, the more dismayed I became. I began to realize how difficult it was for patients in Ohio to get treatment for their obesity. It was also alarming to realize how few Ohio physicians were even willing to treat obesity as the serious disease that it is. Some physicians, in fact, refuse to treat it at all!

But when I began to treat obesity over the Internet, the powerful institutions that control traditional medicine decided to actually *prevent* me from treating the obese. That decision led to the raid described above. Neither the State Pharmacy Board nor the State Medical Board ever called me to request that I quit doing Internet medicine. They did not choose to hold public hearings to determine whether Ohio would accept such a practice. No. Instead, they came into my office with a search warrant, terrorized the office staff, seized my equipment, froze my assets, and further ruined my medical reputation. Then, they took my patients' medical records and started harassing my patients by calling them at home and at work. Suddenly, people who were too embarrassed by their sexual dysfunction to see their regular doctor were being forced to talk with government agents about their medical history! People tend to forget that I worked hard as a physician in the medical community for 15 years. Now all they remember are the current allegations of drug trafficking against me.

The facts about obesity and Internet medicine do not justify the way I have been treated. It is my deepest hope that the information presented in this book will help change attitudes and public perceptions so the serious disease of obesity—in my view, the worst disease in the country—can be treated properly.

PART ONE

OBESITY—THE WORST DISEASE IN THE COUNTRY

OBESITY IS ONE OF MY FAVORITE TOPICS TO DISCUSS. PERHAPS THIS is because I feel an urgent need to dispel the many widespread, irrational myths which surround this serious disease.

Obesity is often found to be rampant in families; recent studies suggest that it can be genetically inherited. Statistics reveal that an individual 100 pounds over his ideal weight has 280 times the risk of dying when compared to a normal-weight individual! Obesity is known to increase your risk of asthma, coronary artery disease, adult-onset diabetes, hypertension, gall bladder disease, various cancers, and more.

As an ER doctor in Ohio, I pronounced dead several hundred people who were markedly overweight. I would also talk to the victim's family after pronouncing the person dead, discussing why their loved one died. I never told these family members "Your loved one died from being overweight." I doubt if other Ohio physicians have done so either. Perhaps I should have. I guarantee you that other physicians throughout this country are also wondering the same thing. However, I believe that I would never have been able to continue working as an ER doctor if I had ever told the family members the truth.

Be honest: what would your response be if a physician came in and told you that your loved one died from being overweight?

Physicians usually tell family members that their loved one had a stroke or heart attack. It would be considered rude, distasteful, improper, and unprofessional to talk about someone's weight problem immediately after they have died. So instead, we avoid discussing obesity as the real cause of someone's death. Families have the right to know that their loved one died from obesity, a deadly disease that kills almost 1,000 people every day or about 300,000 deaths every year.

Many other factors prevent Americans from understanding obesity. This is very ironic considering the prevalence of this disease. Statistics vary, but it is estimated that between thirty and fifty percent of all Americans are obese. Let's take the state of Ohio as an example. Ohio is currently ranked as the fifth most prevalent state for obesity, with 33% of all Ohio residents suffering from it. (South Carolina ranks first, with 34% of its adults being obese.) When ranking the prevalence of obesity in cities, Ohio has three cities included in the top ten nationwide! Cleveland is ranked fifth, Columbus is seventh, and Cincinnati is eighth. Obesity is thus an easy disease to study in Ohio because it is so widespread.

Most physicians still hold that when a patient is overweight, it is there fault! Physicians don't believe that obesity is a disease even though the AMA and U.S. government lists it as such. Instead, many doctors maintain that it is caused from lack of exercise and poor eating habits. Yet most of us know at least one person who is overweight even though he or she consumes very little. Conversely, there are people who can eat, eat, eat and not gain weight. Call it metabolism, call it genetic, call it what you may, but we are not all alike! Indeed, many of us have a disease called obesity.

During the last two years I have personally treated hundreds of obese patients who have told me that their personal physicians had no idea how to treat them; worse yet, these physicians still believed in the myths regarding this serious disease. Not only do these poor people have family physicians who do not understand obesity (or who just refuse to treat it), they also suffer because they live in a state with some of the strictest rules for treating their disease. A full list of Ohio's weight-loss rules is included in Appendix A, but the following discussion of them should help to demonstrate the absurdity of these rules—and the actual danger they pose to patients' lives.

Ohio, regarded as being very conservative, is the only state that does not allow nurse practitioners to write prescriptions without the supervision of a physician. It is also one of the few states where physician assistants cannot write prescriptions. It should therefore come as no surprise to hear that Ohio has very strict rules for physicians to follow, particularly when it comes to weight loss.

The reason for this is that until the early 1980s the mainstay treatment for obesity was a class of medications called amphetamines, commonly referred to as speed. These medications were banned in the 80s because of their addictive nature. However, there had always been other medications besides amphetamines which also worked to treat obesity—it's just that amphetamines worked so well that physicians used them as the first line of treatment. Unfortunately, when Ohio implemented its tough rules on weight loss medications in the 80s because of amphetamines, it also became very conservative in restricting *all* weight-loss medications. As you would expect, as happens with any disease left unchecked, obesity has since flourished in Ohio.

It is my contention that there is a correlation between the prevalence of obesity in Ohio and the strict weight-loss rules devised by the Ohio State Medical Board. It is clear to me that Ohio's weight-loss rules prove beyond a shadow of a doubt that the Ohio State Medical Board does not believe that obesity is really a disease. No other disease even *has* a set of rules which must be followed! The following four facts demonstrate why Ohio's rules suggest that state law incorrectly fails to consider obesity a disease.

1. Unlike other diseases, which can be treated in their early stages, obesity cannot be treated with medications until it has advanced. According to Ohio Revised Code 4731-11-04 (C)(2) [see Appendix A], a patient is not allowed to take weight-loss medications unless he has a Body Mass Index (BMI for short) of 30 or more, even though federal guidelines dictate anyone with a BMI of 25 or more is considered to be overweight. In simple terms, your BMI is calculated using your weight and your height. The higher your BMI, the heavier you are.

   For instance, a 5-foot-tall individual with a weight of

130 pounds has a BMI of 25. If that same person weighed 155 pounds he would have a BMI of 30. Now, if a patient has a co-morbid condition (such as high blood pressure or diabetes) she only needs a BMI of 27 in order to qualify for weight-loss medications in Ohio. Most other states follow the federal government's guidelines of treating those with a BMI of 25 or more—*not 27 to 30*. Thus, a patient who is 5'2" tall would not be able to take weight-loss medications in Ohio until she weighed 164 lbs. Compare that to the 137 lbs. qualifying weight used by the government. A woman who is 5'7" would have to weigh 192 lbs. in order to qualify for weight-loss medications in Ohio. Compare that to the 160 lbs. qualifying weight used by the government. In Ohio, you obviously cannot get your medical treatment early if you are afflicted with obesity. To my knowledge, there is no other such disease in Ohio that cannot be treated in its early stages with medications. In fact, there is no other disease in Ohio where a physician has to follow rules to treat his patients!

2. A twelve-week rule is imposed on certain obesity medications. Certain medications can only be used for twelve weeks in any six-month period for the treatment of obesity. Ohio's justification for this rule is that many older medications only work for twelve weeks. Mind you, the State Medical Board has heard testimony from many weight-loss specialists explaining this myth. (Board minutes are available to the public.) Still, the Board refuses to allow the older medications to be used for more than 12 consecutive weeks. Why? It is because older medications were never given the long-term trials that we now require

with newer medications. However, they honestly do know that the older medications work longer than 12 weeks, since they have been around for so long.

One of these "older medications" is Phentermine, a medication I personally used in my weight-loss centers. I have patient charts that prove that hundreds of Ohio residents continually lost weight on Phentermine for over 12 weeks, because prior to September 1998 there was no 12-week rule. Phentermine is also called Adipex, and many overweight people of our parents' generation used this medication when they were younger! I cannot tell you how discouraging it is for the doctor and patient alike to watch someone successfully lose two to three pounds per week and then have to stop the process after three months because of some ridiculous rule with absolutely no scientific basis. It makes you wonder if someone isn't motivating these Ohio agencies to promote the "new" weight-loss medications and to get rid of the older generic medications that have been used effectively to treat obesity for over 30 years. Pharmaceutical companies will continue to lose millions of dollars every year that Phentermine is available for the treatment of weight loss. Why? Phentermine has no patent anymore and only costs several cents per pill. The newer weight-loss medications go for several dollars per pill and only certain pharmaceutical companies supply them because of patents that have not expired.

3. Ohio requires physicians to stop obesity medication after the disease is under control. Imagine you are an obese person taking medication and finally losing weight. Your

blood pressure has improved, you feel better about yourself, and you're not as winded moving around anymore. Then your doctor says: "I'm sorry, Ms. Jones, but now that you've lost weight and your blood pressure has returned to normal, I'm not giving you any more medication until your blood pressure is high again." This would never happen, right? Wrong! It happens all the time.

No doctor would even dream of taking diabetics off of insulin once their sugar levels became normal. So why would a doctor do the same thing to an obese person? Granted, obese patients may not want to be on weight-loss medications for the rest of their lives; however, people genetically predisposed to obesity will probably face constant, lifelong battles. Yet obese patients in Ohio have no control over the duration of their medication regimen unless they are *markedly* overweight prior to obtaining medical treatment—only then are they allowed to stay on the medication for long-term maintenance. However, when this is the case, the patient must use one of the newer and more expensive medications. And this maintenance treatment must stop if the patient starts gaining back the weight he or she initially lost—a phenomenon most dieters experience from time to time.

4. The physician must physically see obese patients every time they are prescribed weight-loss medications. Obese patients in Ohio are required to see their physician no less than *monthly*. If they miss an appointment without a legitimate excuse, the punishment is that they cannot have any more medication! I find this particular weight-loss rule to be so discriminating that I have a difficult

time understanding how it can even be considered constitutional. Ask any patients with high blood pressure, diabetes, or arthritis if they can only get a one-month supply of their medication per visit to their physicians. They probably see their physicians no more than two times per year. We punish people with obesity, expecting them to see their doctor every four weeks. There is no other disease where we are so cruel to our patients!

The above laws—and these are only a few of the ones I find ridiculous—are listed in full in Appendix A. Such rules should make you question whether the Ohio State Medical Board actually considers obesity a disease.

I find it incredible that no one in Ohio has contested these rules in a court of law. Amazingly, punishment for a physician who fails to follow these rules can be the loss of his or her medical license, when in fact it should be the reverse! Physicians should be punished for *supporting* these rules.

Even according to the most conservative estimates, obesity is killing at least one Ohio resident every day. This is a needless atrocity.

When I first opened my weight-loss centers, I was surprised to find out how emotional—and how rewarding—the giving of care and treatment to patients afflicted with obesity could be. I practiced medicine in emergency rooms for over 10 years and never cried as much as I did while treating my obese patients.

I can't tell you how many times I watched people who were withdrawn, depressed, bitter, and markedly overweight change before my very eyes. I watched people get their lives back. I watched others get a life they never had.

Surprisingly, it is not always the big events that bring happiness to those who lose weight. It is easy to understand how a man or woman who lost 145 pounds in 12 months (and who previously hadn't had a date in five years) would be overjoyed at becoming engaged to be married. In bariatrics, such scenarios happen often. However, sometimes it's the little things that cause joy in a weight-loss patient—things that those of us who have never suffered from obesity take for granted.

For example, I remember a patient who returned from a plane trip and gave me a big hug as soon as I entered the room. Smiling and crying at the same time, she explained that for the first time in several years she had been able to sit in an airplane seat comfortably and to pull down the tray in front of her to eat her meal. She described the humiliation she had always felt previously whenever flight attendants had to bring her a portable tray because she was so large. Maybe this isn't a big deal to someone who has never experienced such humiliation. I can only repeat that I never cried so much while working as a trauma physician (partly because I didn't have time!) as I did when sharing in the joy of my obese patients who had finally received the treatment that helped them successfully lose weight.

Most doctors have no idea what it is like to go through an entire day of office visits and have every patient feel happy to be there. In fact, weight-loss patients are happier and healthier with each new visit they make to your office. Typically, I would see 175 patients during a ten-hour Monday appointment period; it was not unusual to go the entire day without seeing one patient who was unhappy.

Their most common complaint was that it was extremely inconvenient to have to see a physician so often in order to get weight-loss medicine. (By the way, at that time, Ohio required obese patients to be seen every *two* weeks—even now it is still every four weeks!)

Incidentally, I wasn't the only one emotionally affected by my patients' joy. I had a female technician who was tougher than nails. One day she came out of a patient's room crying. When I asked her what was wrong she wouldn't tell me. I went into the patient's room and *she* was crying as well. The patient then shared her elation with me: she had lost over 60 inches and was now able to squeeze into her 14-year-old daughter's pants. Apparently, her daughter used to make fun of her weight and was embarrassed to be with her mom when friends were around. Now, since losing the weight, her daughter had become much closer to her and even asked her mom to chaperone an upcoming dance that weekend. Several weeks later, the daughter accompanied her mother to an appointment and proceeded to personally thank me for giving her back her mom.

I have personally witnessed both men and women lose over fifty pounds and go from being quiet, sad, and introverted to becoming outgoing, happy, and even flirtatious. People don't want to be overweight; they don't remain overweight by personal choice! This is only one of the harmful misconceptions about obesity.

Listed below are five of the most destructive myths about what I call "the worst disease in the country":

1. Obesity is a personal problem caused by eating too much food and can be treated with diet and exercise alone.

2. Medications used to treat obesity are addictive.
3. Medications used to treat obesity are dangerous.
4. Medications do not work to treat obesity because it comes back when the medicine is stopped.
5. Fat is beautiful.

MYTH #1: OBESITY IS A PERSONAL PROBLEM CAUSED BY EATING TOO MUCH FOOD AND CAN BE TREATED WITH DIET AND EXERCISE ALONE.

There was a time (not too terribly long ago, I might add) when people believed that you could get diabetes from eating too much sugar. Even today, some people think you can get high blood pressure from eating too much salt. These are myths. Diabetics do not have diabetes because they eat sweets! Eating sweets can *exacerbate* their diabetes; however, it does not cause it. Likewise, people do not get high blood pressure or hypertension simply because they eat too much salt, although eating too much salt can make hypertension worse. The same logic applies to obesity: people do not get obesity because of eating too much food, although eating too much food can worsen the obesity. Obesity is simply a disease!

If you still have doubts, let me use myself as an example. I love sweets. I eat sweets every day. However, I do not have diabetes. I also love salt and I eat salt on everything. I don't have hypertension either. Many people eat and eat and eat, yet are not obese. We all agree that some people never gain weight no matter how much they eat, and some people just barely look at food and gain weight. Obesity causes death and other related diseases such diabetes, hypertension, heart disease, gall bladder disease, asthma, even cancer. I know I am repeating myself, but I must say it again: obesity is a serious disease and you will not get it from eating too much.

The second part of this myth is that obesity can be treated with diet and exercise alone. The media, by promoting this myth, have really been an enemy of those afflicted with obesity. It amazed me when the news media convinced the entire country to shun Phen-Fen, a drug combination that was saving thousands of lives. They were able to do this without documenting even one death from the use of Phen-Fen—not even one! Negative media coverage, combined with class action suits, destroyed any hope of ever getting Phen-Fen back on the market. Furthermore, the media has the audacity to promote weight loss without the use of *any* medications. Diet and exercise, they say, it's that simple. Well, ask any obese person how many diets he has tried in the past and I bet he says he's tried them all. If only it were that simple! Besides, most patients who are afflicted with obesity are already on diets and exercise. In fact, many obese patients were on diets right up until some physician pronounced them dead!

Let's use the example of diabetes again. Americans would be outraged if someone promoted a non-medical treatment for insulin-dependent diabetics that included diet and exercise but excluded insulin itself. That's different, some might say, because we know insulin-dependent diabetics need insulin. But is it? Research shows that there is a link between obesity and serotonin/dopamine levels in the brain. Medication has been demonstrated to correct chemical imbalances that lead to obesity. Yet many physicians in Ohio still prescribe diet and exercise alone.

I often compare obesity to diabetes because Americans

are very familiar with it. Simply speaking, there are two types of diabetes. Insulin-dependent diabetics need insulin and are classified as Type I diabetics. Type II, non-insulin-dependent diabetes, is the most common form of the disease, with almost 90% of all diabetics classified as Type II. However, insulin is eventually required for many Type II diabetics. Many Type II diabetics are obese and almost 90% of them are believed to have acquired their diabetes because of their associated obesity. In fact, diabetes and heart disease are two of the worst complications of untreated obesity, not including actual death itself.

Let's extend the analogy between diabetes and obesity a bit further. Suppose you have a daughter who has had diabetes for five years and takes insulin shots every day. Now imagine her going to a new doctor because you have just recently moved to Ohio from California. What would you do if that doctor stopped her insulin and told her she wouldn't need it if she just went on a diet and exercise program? At the very least, you would change doctors, knowing your daughter needs her insulin. But what if every doctor in Ohio told you the same thing? You would probably move out of Ohio, especially if you were to learn that Ohio has one of the highest death rates resulting from the disease in this country. You might actually attempt to force Ohio to change its archaic and improper treatment of diabetes. This scenario is exactly what is happening in Ohio in the case of obesity.

Ohio physicians are very willing to treat the *complications* of untreated obesity. In fact, once a patient develops high blood pressure, diabetes, or heart disease, the Ohio doctor will probably be very aggressive with his/her treatment. Only then will they also encourage a patient to lose weight—with (you guessed it) diet and exercise. They might even be audacious enough to suggest to patients that they might not need the blood pressure or diabetes medication if they would *just lose some weight!*

By the way, Ohio actually is also ranked in the top five states for death due to diabetes. No actual death rate per state for obesity exists because physicians, to my knowledge, never sign death certificates with the cause of death listed as obesity. Especially after this book is published, I doubt that any Ohio physician would dare write obesity as the cause of death. Because they refuse to even treat obesity, they obviously would have good reason to fear litigation by the deceased one's heirs.

Obesity should be treated with medication, and I only stress this fact so much because I know all too well the cost of not doing so. While dieting and exercise are both important for improving the health of patients afflicted with hypertension, diabetes, and obesity, they should be used in conjunction with medications.

One final note: some patients do get their obesity under control with diet, exercise, and the use of medication to a point where they *can* eventually stop taking medication; however, the majority of obese patients will have to be on medication most of their lives to treat this deadly disease.

MYTH #2: MEDICATIONS USED TO TREAT OBESITY ARE ADDICTIVE.

This fallacy is based on obsolete practice. Up until the mid-1980s, amphetamines were used to treat obesity. Amphetamines, of course, are very addictive medications—but they have not been used to treat obesity for over ten years!

Two of the most common medications currently used to treat obesity are Phentermine and Meridia™. These medications are still classified as potentially addictive medications even though they are much less addictive than coffee, nicotine, and alcohol. Phentermine has been used to treat obesity for 40 years, while Meridia™ has been on the market for less than 3 years. Unfortunately for Phentermine, its biochemical structure is very similar to that of the amphetamines. Similar, but not the same. This similarity in structure caused Phentermine to be classified as a drug with some potential to be addictive. That classification, however, occurred more than 15 years ago, and has not been revised even though scientists now know that Phentermine has no potential to be abused. Meridia™ also has warnings about its potential for abuse because one of its components is essentially like that of Phentermine. I could cite scientific evidence to make this point; however, common sense arguments often are more powerful.

When something is addictive, it tends to have street value and tends to be abused. Cigarettes and alcohol are two common and readily available substances that can be abused, even though any adult can purchase them. Coffee is also considered addictive and you don't have to be an adult to purchase it. Obviously, these things do not have street value. Then there are the addictive drugs, such as cocaine, marihuana, heroine, crack, and so on, all of which are abused and do have street value. These drugs are illegal and those who sell these drugs are called drug dealers. It should be noted that quite possibly, in the near future, physicians will be allowed to prescribe marihuana in certain states to those patients with chronic illnesses. Physicians already prescribe pain killers such as Talwin, Codeine, Percocet, Percodan, and others, all of which are considered to have street value and can indeed be abused. Phentermine and Meridia™, however, have no street value, according to the drug enforcement agencies of our major cities.

Phentermine, related to Phen-Fen, was taken by millions of people for weight loss in the 90s, but there was never a rash of people experiencing withdrawal from it when it was taken off of the shelves. However, I have seen people experience withdrawal symptoms, sometimes severe, when eliminating caffeine from their diets or when quitting smoking. To my knowledge, not one of my patients has experienced withdrawal symptoms after stopping Phentermine! Not one patient out of over 3,000! This also demonstrates that weight-loss medications are not addictive.

Some physicians and pharmacists may contest this point because, according to the federal Drug Enforcement Agency, Phentermine and Meridia™ are Class IV controlled substances. I believe that these medications will eventually be declassified once the post-1973 studies have been taken into full consideration. Already, a new weight-loss medication called Xenical is being introduced on the market. Because Xenical does not have a structural similarity to amphetamines, it will not be considered addictive from the very outset.

Some prescription medications definitely have the potential for abuse and addiction, but weight-loss medications (excepting amphetamines) are not among them. Drugs such as Darvocet, Tylenol with Codeine, Talwin, Percocet, Percodan, Demerol, and Dilaudid are commonly prescribed and often abused. People with anxiety disorders may be prescribed Xanax, Valium, or other similar medications that are also considered to be extremely addictive. Ritalin, prescribed for children diagnosed with hyperactivity or attention deficit disorder, is an extremely addictive medication, no less so than amphetamines. I find it amazing that so many adults are convinced that weight-loss medications are addictive, while many of them have no problem allowing their children to take Ritalin, a drug that can be taken at age 4!

My point here is twofold. First, addictive amphetamines are not used as weight-loss medication today. Second, the many non-prescription substances such as coffee, nicotine, and alcohol as well as various widely prescribed medications are far more addictive than modern weight-loss medications.

MYTH #3: MEDICATIONS USED TO TREAT OBESITY ARE DANGEROUS.

I must state this firmly to destroy this myth: medications used to treat obesity are *not* dangerous. Obviously, all prescription medicines could be considered dangerous, even though many of them are really very safe! Some may say that if this were true these medications would not require a prescription in the first place. However, it is important to remember how many medications which used to be considered dangerous and required a prescription can now be easily obtained over the counter. What changed? Nothing—except that we have grown older! Over time, many prescription medications have been reclassified as very safe.

Examples of such medications include Monistat for yeast infections, Tinactin for fungal infections, Advil or Motrin for aches and pains, Tavist for congestion, Pepcid and Tagamet for stomach acid build up, and so on. The common Advil, or ibuprofen, in your own medicine cabinet—along with many other medications—used to be available by prescription only! Today, no one thinks twice about administering ibuprofen to himself. It may very well be the case that someday you will be able to get weight-loss medications over the counter at your local grocery store.

Practically speaking, all medications are dangerous if they are abused. Insulin for diabetes can easily kill a careless patient. Blood pressure medications, if taken incorrectly, can do the same. Even aspirin can be considered dangerous if taken in extreme excess.

An excellent example of a dangerous, commonly prescribed medicine is birth control pills. Birth control pills—used as contraceptives, not even as a weapon against disease—are in my opinion one of the most dangerous medications prescribed by physicians. The Physicians' Desk Reference, used to keep track of the different medications on the market by describing a medication's uses, side effects, and contraindications, *actually lists a death chart* in its section on birth control pills. Only the birth control pill section of this reference contains such a chart. These pills are especially dangerous to women smokers but can affect nonsmokers adversely as well. Birth control pills can even cause deadly blood clots in the brain, heart, and lungs. And yet doctors prescribe them for many minor ailments, including irregular periods, cramping, acne, and so on. We as a society commonly accept the prescription of birth control pills even though these contraceptives are immeasurably more dangerous than weight-loss medications.

Weight-loss medications are very safe but have always been misunderstood. Many people, remembering the dangers of amphetamines, still think of weight-loss medications as addictive and dangerous. And, in the case of Phen-Fen, just when patients began to trust weight-loss medications again, this medication was pulled off the market.

The Phen-Fen scare was exactly that—a ridiculous scandal not based on true science or accurate research. A preliminary report scheduled for review in the New England Journal of Medicine suggested a correlation between the use of Phen-Fen and an unusual heart valve abnormality, claiming that up to 33% of Phen-Fen users probably had or would develop this heart valve abnormality. By the way, this was not a study, per se. In this report, which was based on less than 20 cases, a technician observed that some of his obese patients who had been on Phen-Fen had an abnormal heart valve. When the report was broadcast (before the Journal article was published), millions of Phen-Fen users were horrified to hear on national news that Phen-Fen had the potential to cause this particular heart valve problem. Class action suits were also filed against the pharmaceutical companies who marketed Phen-Fen. Almost overnight this media-caused frenzy led to Phen-Fen's removal from the market. The myth that weight-loss medication is dangerous wiped out what, in my opinion, was the best treatment available to patients afflicted with obesity. Even worse, many people with obesity are still afraid to try new medications available thanks to the Phen-Fen scare.

Later Phen-Fen studies never demonstrated a correlation between Phen-Fen and these heart valve problems. In fact, newer reports indicate that Phen-Fen was not that dangerous after all: heart valve problems were far less prevalent than initially thought and were in fact reversible when

Phen-Fen was stopped. More importantly, obesity itself was found as a cause of heart valve abnormalities. Other medications currently available such as Meridia™ and Xenical are considered even safer than the Phen-Fen combination, but the damage has been done. The media reinforced the myth that weight-loss medications are dangerous.

That false accusation of danger prevented millions of patients with obesity from taking a medication combination that was safe and very effective. The media pat themselves on the back for supposedly saving 5,000 lives annually by getting Phen-Fen off the market. But there is no proof that these deaths due to Phen-Fen ever would have occurred.

We do, however, have proof that people die from obesity—as many as 300,000 a year. Why do the media ignore the hundreds of thousands of deaths caused annually by obesity and yet inflate the dangers of medications that address this tragedy? Like many physicians, our media do not recognize obesity as a serious disease. What else could explain such interest in *potential* deaths caused by Phen-Fen and such lack of interest in the *actual* deaths caused by obesity?

I believe it is immoral to prevent anyone afflicted with obesity from being able to readily obtain weight-loss medications when the risk of taking the medicine is far less than the risk of letting obesity go untreated. The dangers of untreated obesity outweigh those caused by the medications that effectively treat it. But common sense seems to be abandoned when it comes to weight-loss medications.

MYTH #4: MEDICATIONS DO NOT WORK TO TREAT OBESITY BECAUSE THE WEIGHT COMES BACK WHEN THE MEDICINE IS STOPPED.

Obesity is a chronic, lifelong disease that needs to be treated in the same manner as other chronic diseases. Medication, in combination with diet, exercise, and lifestyle changes will often keep this deadly disease at bay. Sometimes, as with other diseases, the medication can be halted. Some non-insulin-dependent diabetics, as well as some patients with mild hypertension, can get along well without medication once their disease is under control. Similarly, some people on weight-loss medication can stop taking their medications once the disease is under control. However, they are the exceptions rather than the rule. Unfortunately, most people with obesity will need to remain on medication for the rest of their lives. This is not a flaw in the medications but simply an unfortunate condition of their use.

MYTH #5: FAT IS BEAUTIFUL. (PLEASE DON'T BE OFFENDED—READ ON!)

I am not referring here to whether a person is attractive—in fact I don't particularly like using the word "fat." But I emphasize this myth to stress how difficult it can be for obese people to live a normal life in this country.

Many obese Americans are faced with discrimination and prejudice. It is tougher for someone afflicted with obesity to get a job, a promotion, a date, or even to receive medical treatment. Unlike diabetes, hypertension, heart disease, or sexual dysfunction, there is no visible way of hiding obesity—it is apparent to all. Even children can make the diagnosis.

Discrimination is supposed to be illegal; however, it occurs around us all the time. Unfortunately, some doctors, insurance companies, and even state agencies continue to discriminate against the obese. Doctors may refuse to prescribe weight-loss medication, and even when they do prescribe it certain insurance companies may then refuse to cover its cost. Finally, state agencies make weight-loss rules so strict and confusing that doctors are afraid of not being able to adhere to them. I can't help but feel this is an ugly world at times for those who are afflicted with obesity—not beautiful!

Statistics suggest that in Ohio 33% of any family doctor's patients are probably in some stage of obesity. If Ohio is ranked fifth in the nation with the incidence of obesity, then Ohio physicians should be treating obesity—in fact, it is highly unethical not to. Realistically, Ohio's physicians should have their hands full treating all of these clients. However, judging from my weight-loss patients' claims to the contrary, I am certain this is not the case. Many of my patients came to my center for help only *after* being denied treatment from their family doctor.

When obesity is left untreated, patients often develop other medical problems: hypertension, gallbladder disease, adult onset diabetes, asthma, cancer, or heart disease just to name a few. Numerous studies suggest that these complications could be prevented if the patient's obesity had been alleviated in the first place. Personally, I feel that refusing to treat obesity is as immoral as refusing to treat hypertension or diabetes. I am also quite certain that it could be considered malpractice. I know that if a doctor refused to treat any other disease, his career would be a short one. I can only guess that Ohio residents allow the refusal of treatment to continue because they have never been informed that obesity really is considered a deadly disease, one that deserves aggressive treatment. I hope this book will drastically change Ohio's position on how to treat obesity. I feel strongly that Ohio needs to be more in line with the rest of this country concerning weight-loss rules and regulations. It is time to point a finger at those people who are in a position of authority and ask them to behave responsibly. It is time for Ohio residents to demand that these rules be changed.

Not only must physicians be held liable for failing to treat obesity; the state Medical and Pharmacy Boards must be held accountable as well. The above-mentioned Ohio agencies have chosen to go against the national norm with regard to the definition of what obesity is and how it should be treated. In October of 1998, the State Medical Board and State Pharmacy Board made the treatment of obesity tougher than almost every other state in the nation. (See Appendix A.) I have personally heard one State Pharmacy Board investigator say that he didn't really think obesity was a disease. He told me this during a conversation we were having when he returned the medical records that were confiscated during the search of my office.

In Ohio, physicians cannot treat obesity until it has become severe. That's right—patients are turned away because they are not heavy enough. You may be 3 pounds under the minimum requirement and refused treatment to lose those extra 50 pounds you're carrying around. Unfortunately, this isn't an exaggeration. Common sense tells us that it is easier to take off as little as 5 extra pounds than to allow the weight to accumulate to an excessive amount. I had a patient who was gaining approximately 10 pounds every month before coming to my weight-loss center. The reason for this was unclear. She started taking weight-loss medication and subsequently gained only one pound during each of the next two months. Because she gained, however, I was required by Ohio law to stop her medication. Ohio weight-loss rules require you to cease taking weight-loss medication if you gain weight for two consecutive months. My patient was devastated because the medication had obviously decreased the rate of her weight gain.

It is absurd that many good physicians have lost their medical licenses because they broke Ohio's unfair weight-loss rules. Ideally, a physician who has lost his or her license in Ohio for responsibly treating obesity should be rewarded, not punished.

This horribly unjust situation can be changed, but only if obesity—not only in Ohio, but everywhere—is taken seriously. The best ways to get the attention of the state agencies responsible for unjust weight-loss regulations are political action, financial pressure, and media coverage.

First, the political channels. Ohio State Medical Board members are appointed for five-year terms by the Governor. Pharmacy Board members are either appointed or elected by Ohio residents. I suggest a letter-writing campaign to these agencies. We all ought to communicate to our government officials about the need for action to change these rules. As for physicians, they should demand the freedom to treat weight loss by contacting all of the medical organizations and societies where they pay dues.

Financial leverage could include legal action. Attorneys can file class action suits on behalf of the families of any Ohio patients afflicted with obesity who were denied treatment and/or who subsequently died from an obesity-related disease. Attorneys should also offer class action suits for those physicians who have lost their medical licenses while trying to treat obesity in Ohio. I also suggest that people organize a non-profit group to fight this battle nationwide. We could call it something such as "The American Obesity Foundation."

Finally, I would like to see the media redeem themselves with regard to their role in obesity treatment. We need to educate people throughout the country about how serious and deadly a disease obesity can be. I recommend that the media nationwide interview agencies which treat obesity as the dangerous disease it really is. We must draw attention to the agencies responsible for making strict weight-loss rules. It will become obvious that these agencies are really uninformed when it comes to the disease known as obesity and the relative safety of the medications available to treat this serious disease. I suggest the media also interview patients afflicted with obesity to get their perspective on how difficult it is to get appropriate treatment. I think you'll find that if we as citizens put financial, political, and media pressure on these agencies, we will collectively be able to change one of the largest medical travesties that patients have had to endure.

Diet and exercise are simply not enough. We need to stop promoting them as *the* simple cure. Rather, we have a moral obligation to promote medication *in conjunction with* diet and exercise, just as we do for hypertension or diabetes. Help me help Ohio change how obesity is viewed and treated by both doctors and laypeople in this country.

PART TWO

Internet Medicine

LIKE OBESITY, INTERNET MEDICINE IS SURROUNDED BY MANY myths. As with any technology, preconceptions can make people fear a practice which one day everyone will take for granted as natural, convenient, and ordinary. I believe this will soon be the public perception of Internet medicine.

I am frequently asked the following question: "How can you give prescription medications to people without actually examining them?"

My answer is as follows: First of all, physicians have been prescribing medications to patients without doing an examination for many years—long before we had the Internet. Secondly, an examination is often useless. Third, many of my patients have already been examined by a physician and already know what is wrong with them. Finally, some medical problems are so obvious that children can make the diagnosis. A patient does not need a physician to tell her she is suffering from obvious problems. Internet medicine can do a good job of serving many patients if traditional medicine practitioners can accept it as a positive reality rather than a threat.

Traditional medicine has changed dramatically over the twentieth century. We have all heard stories of physicians in the old days who were reimbursed with food or products for their services. House calls were the norm at one time. As technology progressed, physicians changed their medical practices so that they could have more time for personal activities. Unlike the physicians of the past, today's physicians can work 30 to 50 hours per week and take two to six weeks of vacation every year. This has become possible because of technology. Hospitals, nurses, technicians, monitors, beepers, faxes, x-rays, laboratories, medicines, and increased numbers of physicians all have contributed to more free time for physicians. Ironically, physicians actually work fewer hours and, relatively speaking, make more money than their predecessors did.

When I was growing up, the only time anyone ever went to see the physician was when that person was sick. An appointment would be made for later that same week or that same day if the illness seemed serious. The doctor examined you and wrote you a prescription to be filled at the pharmacy. That is not the typical scenario for someone needing medical treatment today. Today, traditional medicine is best described by what I call the "fair weather" doctor. Internet medicine is getting ready to replace many of those physicians who have enjoyed their "fair weather" medical practices.

Physicians can be like banks and many so-called friends. They are always there when you don't need them and never around when you do need them. Patients are expected to fit their illnesses around the physician's schedule. Often, because physicians are not available when needed, appointments must be scheduled months in advance. If you are sick, heaven forbid, physicians tell you to go to the emergency room, where you must wait for hours to be treated by some physician who has never seen you before!

When patients do have scheduled appointments, why must they wait so long after arriving to be seen? The answer is sadly very obvious: physicians don't care about your schedule! What are you going to do . . . leave? After you have waited months to get in to see your physician, it is very doubtful that you will leave because of the wait!

Did you know there are good and bad times to get sick? In an emergency room, you are much better off having your heart attack during daylight hours on weekdays than if you have your heart attack on weekends or nights. The same cardiologist who would be very aggressive during a weekday and do emergency procedures on heart attack victims will, more likely than not, send nighttime and weekend heart attack victims to the intensive care unit to "be watched." Orthopedic surgeons will operate on weekdays but often schedule weekend injuries to be fixed during the week. They will splint broken bones at night and on weekends. Many of those same patients would have had surgery immediately if they had simply had their injury on a weekday during daytime hours. Not all physicians are this way, but at least half of the physicians I have worked with are definitely much more aggressive during the weekday daytime hours than at all other times.

One last piece of advice: never get sick and end up in the hospital during the first week of July. Why? The new interns start! Your doctor may have less than 30 hours of actual experience as a medical doctor during the first week of July. This should not be true. The reason you get stuck with the new intern in July is because the more experienced upperclassmen are off. Oh, there will be an upperclassman supervising all those new interns. However, it will be his first month in such a supervisory position. The further a resident gets in his residency, the more free time he has to do other things. An intern can expect to be on call every third or fourth night, while upperclassmen may only take call every fifth to seventh night. From the very beginning of their training, physicians learn the importance of having time off.

Let us proceed to dissect the fair-weather physician even further. What is the usefulness of a doctor when you actually do get to see one? For example, you are going to see your physician for an annual examination. What does the physician do when you get to his office? First, you give the receptionist your insurance information (if you have insurance) and wait for your doctor to see you. Usually, a nurse or technician will see you first and do some essentials like taking your blood pressure, weight, possibly blood work and EKG, taking a history of why you are there. At last, the physician comes in.

What does the physician actually do when he examines you? A good physician will take a medical history and follow this with a physical examination. But here is where my primary quarrel with traditional medicine begins: as a practicing physician for over 15 years, I can assure you that the routine physical examination is nearly worthless. Many physicians know this but deny it.

Let me place two qualifications on this assertion. First, the examination is not worthless if the patient has come in with a vague complaint. Secondly, the taking of vital signs (blood pressure, pulse, breathing rate, or temperature) is not worthless either—but it does not require a highly trained physician to check vital signs. Treating patients over the Internet makes perfect sense once the ineffectiveness of physical examinations is proven, as I will show in the following pages.

Clearly, physical examinations are not highly valued in traditional medicine. Hospitals hire nurses to do pre-admission examinations on patients being admitted. Many specialists also have their nurses perform the examinations for their hospitalized patients. University hospitals have medical students do the patient examinations; the attending physician merely adds what is called a physician note. Insurance companies utilize technicians to do insurance examinations. Such a low priority of routine physical examinations demonstrates that it they are of very little use most of the time. Again, I am not talking about the examination done on a patient with difficulty breathing or belly pain. I am talking about the routine examinations done every year on millions of patients who have no complaints.

As for taking vital signs, any high school student can be taught to take someone's pulse, blood pressure, respiratory rate, and temperature. In fact, there are machines in many pharmacies, grocery stores, and malls that will take a person's blood pressure and pulse. Thus, there is no reason why people in this country need to see a physician to see if they have high blood pressure. Even in most of the patients who present with a particular complaint, it is the history that usually gives the physician his clues. The lab, X-rays, EKG, and other tests finally make the diagnosis.

Let's consider another example: the female examination. Women know that many physicians do far too thorough a female examination than is needed for non-female related complaints! Pelvic examinations and breast examinations should only be done with a nurse present and should take less than 5 minutes. They should be done when requested or when pertinent. They should not be done for sore throats, ear aches, colds, cough—you get the picture!

Now let's look at appendicitis—a great example of how worthless the physical examination can be. I have seen some of the best physicians money can buy miss the diagnosis of appendicitis because they think they can recognize it with the physical examination. I have seen many more great physicians miss the diagnosis because they relied on blood tests, temperature, appetite, and X-rays, combined with the physical examination. Appendicitis cannot be diagnosed by examination. Ask any attorney who specializes in malpractice claims and he will agree with me.

In physical examinations what does the physician use his stethoscope for anyway? It is used to listen to the lungs, heart, and sometimes the belly. It can also be used to take blood pressures, but physicians rarely take blood pressures. Most of the time, a patient's blood pressure is taken by a nurse, a technician, or an automated machine. Did you know that most physicians could not diagnose classic pneumonia with their stethoscope? The same goes for partially collapsed lungs, lung tumors, small heart murmurs, and so on. The stethoscope examination is very useful for things like heart failure, asthma, and large murmurs—things often so obvious that the layperson can identify them. When a child has an asthmatic attack, the parents don't need a stethoscope to tell what is going on!

So what, really, does the physician pick up on the physical examination? To be perfectly honest, almost nothing. Most of the time the only reason a physician finds something unusual on the examination is because the patient pointed out the abnormality in the first place (for example, "Doc, what is that bump there?" or "Look at this," or "Is this normal?").

Let's say you see your doctor because you have a sore throat. Your doctor does an examination that reveals you have puss in your tonsils. Your own examination was limited because you could not see your tonsils. He does a throat culture and it does not reveal a strep infection, so he does not treat you with antibiotics. Did you know that cultures of the throat miss up to 20% of strep throat infections? Maybe not, but your doctor should know this. Let's go one step further and suppose you get strep infections at least four times a year and now have the typical pain and red throat you get when you have these infections. Do you really need a doctor to make your diagnosis and prescribe antibiotics for you? Worse yet, suppose you go to all the trouble to see your doctor for your typical strep throat and he decides it is just a "cold" and refuses to give you antibiotics!

When you have a specific complaint, your doctor will do more than just examine you. He will do other tests as well. When you don't have any specific complaints, his examination will most likely be a waste of time. It is actually the blood tests, urine tests, CT scans, EKGs, X-rays, stress tests, and so on that are most important in making a diagnosis.

Not surprisingly, they also are the moneymakers for your doctor. In fact, your doctor often knows how to treat you without ever doing a physical examination! He ascertains all the essential information from the medical history taken by his nurse or technician.

Doctors around the country will disagree with these statements about the physical examination, but I am right and they are just being defensive. The same physicians who claim that the examination is a very important part of a patient's medical evaluation will allow nurses and technicians to do this examination for them—and then charge the patient's insurance $70-120 for an examination they didn't even perform. Have you ever been hospitalized and had several physicians come in and see you during your hospital stay only to find, after going home, that you get billed by all of these physicians who never even examined you? Physicians believe the examination is critical for diagnosing patients simply because that belief is critical for their financial well being.

Several years ago, a 25-year-old non-drug-using man was pronounced dead in an emergency room where I worked. He had seen his family physician and three ER physicians during the two weeks prior to his death. His reason for seeing all of these doctors was "chest pain." He had blood work, EKGs, X-rays, and more, but still died at the age of 25! Why? He needed a heart catheterization to determine if he had any heart vessel disease. This is a specialized procedure where a special dye is injected into the blood vessels around the heart to see if any of them have blockage from disease or blood clots. He did not have this done because everyone figured he was too young to have heart disease. Four physical examinations did nothing to save his life.

Most doctors today know better than to rely on physical examinations because if they do not order tests they can be sued later. Missed fractures or missed broken bones are one of the most common malpractice suites charged against physicians because some physicians still think they can tell if something is broken without using X-rays. Pneumonia is another frequently missed diagnosis which results in patient malpractice litigation because the doctor did not do an X-ray. Physicians still think that they can hear pneumonia, and that if they don't hear it must not be present. Lawyers love this mentality!

The routine annual examination could easily be replaced by monthly vital signs. Blood work to check cholesterol, sugar, potassium, and so on could be done every year or two, depending on the patient's age and current health status. Then a more thorough investigation could be done when someone has a physical complaint or an abnormal blood test. A technician rather than a physician could easily be used in this process. Obviously, this reality is a threat to the livelihoods of physicians and to the entire medical establishment.

Technological advances are already starting to replace the physician. Via tele-medicine, a physician can now examine a patient who is hundreds of miles away. In fact, astronauts in outer space were even monitored medically via tele-medicine. Radiologists can now view X-rays from home via their computer monitors without ever going to the office or hospital. Medicine today is already being practiced from a distance by means of these and other new technologies.

In fact, technology alone can perform tasks which used to

require a physician's presence. Heart monitors can now diagnose irregular heart rhythms and actually give electrical shocks to those hearts that need it. Heart patients can even wear jackets with built-in heart monitors and computers that will shock the heart when necessary. Internal pacemakers now can recognize heart arrhythmias and internally defibrillate or shock the patient's heart. Cardiologists used to do stress tests and special invasive heart procedures called heart catheterizations to determine if a patient had coronary heart disease, but now sophisticated CAT scans can pick up early coronary blockage without stress tests or invasive procedures. Computers can administer medications through intravenous lines into patients at appropriate times throughout a patient's hospital stay.

Think about the typical training required for a physician to practice medicine. He studies anatomy, diseases, how the body works, and how to treat disease using medications and behavior modification. But today, computers can administer treatment far better than physicians. Computers can even be programmed to read X-rays better than radiologists, or pathology slides better than pathologists. Pap smears to detect cervical cancer are now being read by computers rather than pathologists because they can do it faster and with fewer errors. Some ultrasound machines can detect sounds physicians can not even hear. Technological innovations are already outdistancing the traditional physician.

Ultrasound provides a good example of how much medicine is performed today by technicians—without the aid of a physician. A technician can put jelly on your skin and not only hear sounds but also see pictures that are generated to help make decisions about what is wrong with someone.

Technicians can easily do a patient's examination and, if they find anything unusual, can order further tests. The results of examinations could be input into computers, which could even tell technicians what other tests should be done. Computers can actually give you the final diagnosis and treatment plan. Such developments have already become reality.

I was a trauma emergency room physician for over 10 years. In that setting, time is of the essence. Life is lost when delays occur in finding out what is wrong with a trauma patient. I always said that there would come a day when trauma patients would be passed through a total body scan immediately after arriving in the trauma room. The scan would be computerized and any abnormalities would be detected by the scan and printed out on a screen or printer. That technology, a total body CT scan, is now being used in some trauma centers in this country for diagnosing trauma injuries! Technology is taking away the jobs or responsibilities that used to be the physician's responsibility.

With technology's greater influence, physicians are already being replaced by physician assistants and nurse practitioners throughout the country. The only physicians not threatened thus far are those with a technical skill that cannot be reproduced by a machine or computer. But even specialists with technical skills are not immune to being replaced by new technology. Surgeons do biopsies and surgeries with scalpels. They could soon be replaced by technicians or computers, which, instead of using scalpels to operate and needles to obtain biopsies, perform these tasks with lasers. We now use glue to repair skin lacerations and staples for those lacerations that are under increased tension. Who would have ever thought that a doctor would request a staple gun and glue to treat a patient with multiple lacerations? This is common practice in most emergency rooms in this country today. Do you really think a technician can't learn to use a staple gun or glue?

No matter how much physicians will disagree, it is obvious that fewer physicians will be needed in the 21st century as technological advances continue. Those physicians still around will have a more supervisory role; technicians, machines, and computers will do most of the legwork. The ability to have your own personal physician is soon to be a thing of the past—it is already happening.

Remember when a physician knew not only all of his patients but their families as well? This was before physicians started seeing more patients in less time. This was before managed care, when HMOs and PPOs began determining which doctors people were allowed to see according to the restrictions of an insurance policy. Nowadays it is quite typical to find that most people don't really have a particular doctor they see when they are sick or well. Instead, they see some doctor who is covering for the doctor who was on their insurance card the last time they became ill. Their doctor is often a stranger; many times they have never seen him or her personally! Some patients are even forced to stop seeing their regular physician because he or she was not covered in their current health plans.

Is it any wonder that thousands of Americans have been looking for safe alternatives by which they can receive their medical care? An outstanding alternative has arrived—one which threatens to destroy the very fragile existence of traditional medicine. It is called Internet medicine.

Internet medicine is the most threatening type of medical practice that traditional physicians have ever seen. This threat stems from the fact that routine medical treatments will be available to patients without them ever having to see their regular physician.

To help you understand this threat better, consider what would happen to physicians if patients did not need prescriptions to obtain medicine. In Europe patients obtain most of their medications without a prescription and physicians there don't make nearly as much money as their American counterparts for that very reason. Antibiotics like erythromycin and penicillin are over-the-counter medicines in Europe. So is Viagra™ in some countries. As mentioned earlier, even in this country many of the medicines that you can now buy over the counter (Monistat, Tinactin, Advil, Tavist, Tagamet) used to be prescription-only medications.

Physicians will tell you that it is too dangerous to let patients decide when they need medications. Besides, patients would not know what medication to take. For instance, people would abuse antibiotics and take them when they are not indicated. This would put those people at risk for what we call super infections; infections caused by bacteria which are resistant to many antibiotics and cannot be killed. If that is true, then why hasn't that happened in Europe? The more obvious explanation is that doctors don't want you to be able to get your medications without seeing them because they will lose money.

When your child gets swimmer's ear for the thousandth time you don't need your physician to tell you he has swimmer's ear; you would buy the drops at the grocery store if they were available. Every fall you develop bronchitis and your doctor prescribes an antibiotic that makes you better; obviously, you would get that antibiotic from your local grocery store if you could. When your daughter runs out of inhaler for her asthma, you would certainly buy that at the grocery store as well if you could. I could list an entire book full of practical examples where patients would never choose to see a physician if they could get their medication without a prescription.

Up till now, physicians have been very successful in maintaining control over their patients' medical treatment. According to law, patients need prescriptions to get their medications. This legal framework of control has allowed physicians to maintain lucrative practices where patients are totally dependent on the physician for their medical care. That control will soon become obsolete because of technology, technicians, and Internet medicine.

Internet medicine is really about giving patients more control with regards to their medical treatment. Most of the time, patients do not need a physician to tell them what is wrong with them or what medicine is needed to treat their problem. They already know this. Often, all patients need is a simple and convenient method to obtain their prescription medication. Internet medicine provides patients with a method to obtain medical treatment without being under the strict schedule their regular physician mandates. In fact, Internet medicine allows many patients to discontinue making those absurd office visits to physicians who are really doing nothing more than approving their prescriptions anyway for an antibiotic, ear drops, or perhaps even a simple refill of a medicine already being taken on a regular basis. Internet medicine allows patients the ability to order their medicine anytime without having to make an appointment. The medication is then shipped to their home or office within 48 hours.

The traditional physician cannot compete with this type of convenience for those routine office visits. Physicians who lose this aspect of their office practice will experience a marked decrease in their personal revenue. So, do not expect to ever hear anything positive about Internet medicine from your family physician—unless of course, he also provides an Internet site for his own patients!

I grew up in a very small town in South Dakota, where it was a 15 to 25 mile drive to the nearest doctor's office. Believe me, no one went to the doctor's office unless he was really sick. I think that is how it should be! You don't need to see a physician to have your cholesterol, triglycerides, blood pressure, or your sugar checked. You should be able to have these tests done without needing to see a doctor. In fact, you can have these tests done by chiropractors, insurance technicians, and many labs for a nominal fee.

I first entered the world of Internet medicine in September of 1998 when I began offering Viagra™ to patients throughout this country. Our attorneys' research determined that no regulations had yet been drafted restricting this activity and that it would be at least three years before any specific regulations appeared.

Since Internet medicine was legal, I then had to determine if it was safe. My review of Viagra™ from all sources indicated that the only people who should not take Viagra™ were those with heart problems and those on nitrates or nitroglycerine. Other websites which were selling Viagra™ on the Internet provided an excellent review of how Viagra™ worked, what its side effects were, what medications cannot be taken with Viagra™, and how to take it. These sites were very thorough. The medical histories they required were very complete. Obviously, the only thing the sites did not provide was a physical examination.

But a physical examination is worthless with regards to prescribing Viagra™! Every good doctor knows that heart disease is undetectable by examination. Oh sure, you can detect murmurs and high blood pressure, but not coronary heart disease. Furthermore, Viagra™ is used to treat sexual dysfunction; a diagnosis physicians cannot possibly make with a physical examination.

In addition, it can be embarrassing for patients to answer questions asked by nurses and technicians, to discuss their sexual dysfunction with the physician, and then to hand their prescription to a pharmacist who may ask many questions and explain side effects of the medications the patient is receiving. Often, other people are waiting in line to get their medication, some of them perhaps acquaintances of the patient, and they are likely to overhear the pharmacist discussing Viagra™. Compare that scenario with getting a medication via the Internet after a totally private ten-minute medical consultation and application completed on a computer at the patient's convenience. Thanks to Internet medicine, Viagra™ could be sent to a patient's home or office within 48 hours of ordering.

The more I got to thinking about Internet medicine, the more I realized that it would change how medicine is practiced forever.

Shortly after I began offering Viagra™ on the Internet, I started thinking of other medications that would be safe to offer patients via the Internet. Obviously, such medications should treat medical problems that were common and could be diagnosed without actually seeing a physician. It didn't take me long to come up with a short list of medical problems and some standard medications used to treat each of them:

Smoking . . . . Zyban
Baldness . . . . Propecia
Recurrent Genital Herpes . . . . Valtrex
Sexual dysfunction . . . . Viagra

I soon offered all of these medications to people throughout the country. *None of these medications has any contraindication that can be discerned from a physical examination!* Only the medical history of the patient can determine a patient's eligibility for the above medications.

It quickly became obvious that many people in this country prefer an Internet medicine consultation to visiting their own physician. They were willing to pay a premium to have the convenience and privacy of the Internet, even when many of them had insurance that would have covered a visit to their own physician.

And so in December, 1998, I decided to offer weight-loss treatment via the Internet. There were already physicians offering weight-loss treatment on the Internet, a practice that had been occurring for several years. One physician had patients not only throughout the U.S. but even internationally. Some websites from other countries even offered weight-loss medications to Americans without a medical consultation or a physician involved! Our own attorneys had told us that the only problem with Internet medicine was that certain states could request that we discontinue this service in their state. They also asked us why we were not doing weight loss on the Internet, since that was definitely my area of expertise!

Naturally, I became very excited about the possibility of offering weight-loss medications on the Internet for patients afflicted with obesity. Physical examinations had never proved useful in my own weight-loss practice. Over a two-year period, I had treated over 3,000 patients in my weight-loss centers without ever disqualifying a patient from using medication because of something I found on physical examination. The other physician who took over my weight-loss centers agreed with me—no physical examination ever caused him to disqualify any of the 2,000-plus patients whom he treated for weight loss.

The only physical finding that could contraindicate the use of weight-loss medications is the blood pressure reading. Remember that most physicians don't even take blood pressure readings, and you don't have to see a physician to have your blood pressure checked. Most workplaces have a health nurse who will check your blood pressure, and all emergency/fire stations have personnel who can do so. Grocery stores, pharmacies, and shopping malls have machines that will take your blood pressure automatically.

Thus, I added obesity to the list of medical problems for which we offered treatment via our Internet medicine practice. We decided not to offer weight-loss medications to Ohio addresses on our Internet site because we felt it would be a conflict of interest from a business standpoint. We had been running weight-loss centers in Ohio for two years and had franchises across Ohio. Even though our weight-loss centers were failing because of the State Medical Board's strict weight-loss rules, we did not want anyone to blame our Internet success for our weight-loss center's failure. Ohio's weight-loss rules were so strict, in fact, that many patients traveled to other states—usually Kentucky and West Virginia—to obtain medication when they could no longer receive it from Ohio physicians. These states allowed physicians to treat patients with weight-loss medications even though they were out-of-state residents.

I planned to find non-Ohio physicians to join my Internet medicine practice so that I could offer weight-loss treatments to Ohio residents via the Internet. I wanted physicians who were licensed in other states to join me so that my practice could continue if any one state declared that physicians in that state could no longer practice Internet medicine. Our goal was to start a company subsidiary that was associated with our regular weight-loss centers, but which offered Internet access to those Ohio residents interested. However, our clinics were failing quickly, so if we didn't find another physician soon it would be too late to save our conventional centers. We would still be able to provide Internet access to Ohio, even if I could not find another physician before our centers failed.

And so we opted to delay treating obesity in Ohio via the Internet initially. We even added a flashing banner to my web sites stating that weight-loss medications were not available at this time for Ohio residents. Ironically, I could treat patients afflicted with obesity throughout the rest of the country on my Internet site, but I avoided treating Ohio residents even though they were some of those who needed it most!

Needless to say, hundreds of people with obesity throughout the U.S. became my Internet patients in several short weeks. In less than 45 days, I had over 1,000 patients afflicted with obesity being served by my Internet practice. I had many requests from Ohio residents for treatment, even though the site clearly stated that Ohio was off limits. Because of the growing pains of a new business, combined with an administrative error, I did treat one or two Ohio residents with obesity over the Internet: several Ohio residents received weight-loss medications even though they gave us Ohio addresses. I consider one or two cases not bad, considering that hundreds of Ohio residents with Ohio addresses were requesting treatment.

I specifically remember one Ohio resident who did receive weight-loss medications from me during the first several weeks we offered them. One evening while I was reviewing that day's orders I noted that one of the male weight-loss patients whom I had approved earlier that day had an Ohio address. My staff usually voided all Ohio orders, but somehow they had inadvertently missed this one. I thought about canceling his order after it had been sent, calling him to say that we didn't want to do Ohio weight-loss over the Internet. But I didn't call him for several reasons. First, he was located in a part of Ohio where we had no regular weight-loss centers. This meant he wasn't likely to personally or through word of mouth cause any loss of revenue to our regular weight-loss centers or those of our franchises. Secondly, this patient was a man; my experience with Ohio weight-loss patients indicated that men are less likely to seek treatment for their disease because they are embarrassed and they don't have the time to come into the office. Later, that same Ohio resident's brother also ordered weight-loss medications and I filled his prescription as well. I was happy to see two males taking weight-loss medications, and I knew that people are more successful in losing weight if they have support from another family member. In this way, several people with Ohio addresses did manage to get their obesity treated via my Internet sites.

By February I had two non-Ohio physicians ready to join my practice, but I needed to get an online pharmacy going so that the physicians I hired could use that pharmacy for their patient's prescriptions. I requested an application from the Ohio State Pharmacy Board for a pharmacy license so that we could start an online pharmacy complete with pharmacists. Our company was advertising in newspapers, magazines, and on the Internet. I was getting ready to hire additional physicians, start my own Internet pharmacy, and initiate taking the steps necessary to take my company public when we had the unexpected "visit" described in this book's introduction.

I was shocked and dismayed to learn from the search warrant submitted to me on that February 17th that two people from Ohio had received weight-loss medications from us via the Internet. Out of all the Ohio residents afflicted with obesity whom I refused, the two "brothers" were members of the Ohio State Pharmacy Board requesting a medicine they didn't even need! The upshot is that two administrative slip-ups in which my heart went out to two people claiming to need obesity medication got me indicted and could cost me my practice.

✴✴✴

Ohio's State Pharmacy Board is trying to stop Internet medicine by making it illegal. Even though no laws regarding Internet medicine are currently on the books, I am being criminally charged for practicing Internet medicine. Remember that I spent a lot of money having Internet medicine researched to make sure that it was *not* illegal. Although Internet medicine has not been prohibited here, Ohio has taken the stance that it should be. As I see it, the state plans to use me as a guinea pig in order to get Internet medicine banned. If the state wins, then every other state in this country can use this Ohio case to ban Internet medicine nationwide.

Talk about putting the cart before the horse! Would any physician risk imprisonment and the loss of his medical career if he knew Internet medicine were already illegal? Here is an analogous situation: We used to have a speed limit of 70 miles per hour in this country. Now it is 65 miles per hour. No one had to be indicted for this change in the speed limit to take effect. Likewise, there was no need for the Ohio State Pharmacy Board to ruin my credibility, threaten my career and freedom, and force me to spend several hundred thousand dollars in legal fees just to make Internet medicine illegal.

The common disregard for the laws regulating how traditional physicians write prescriptions for patients is the heart of the matter in my case. No physician follows our current prescription laws and no pharmacy boards enforce these rules; for this reason, it is ludicrous to consider making Internet medicine illegal.

Let's explore these rules which physicians are supposed to

follow in order to write prescriptions for their patients. I am being accused of criminal activity because I do not follow these rules when I practice Internet medicine, but I believe that in order to prosecute me for not following the rules discussed below, the State Pharmacy Board would also have to prosecute over 90% of all Ohio physicians.

Here are two rules that have been on the books for years and yet are rarely taken seriously by either physicians or the pharmacy board:

1. Prescribing dangerous medications by a physician without an examination is illegal.
2. Prescribing medications without a face-to-face visit between the patient and the physician is illegal.

The state of Ohio thus contends that Internet medicine does not allow the physician to provide the minimum standard of care compared to other physicians treating similar ailments or diseases.

On the surface this sounds reasonable! There was a time when physicians really did examine patients before prescribing medications. But when was that? I am not certain except that I know it was before I became a physician in 1983. Since I received my medical degree in 1983, physicians have frequently prescribed medications to people they never saw in person, let alone examined.

During my residency, we were taught that it is acceptable to call in prescriptions for patients that we talk with by telephone. We often called in prescriptions for patients whom we never saw in our private clinics. We also gave verbal orders to nurses daily with regards to medications we wanted called in for various patients. When we started taking call for one another it was even more common. I remember covering for five to seven other physicians during my residency on some weekends. I would get calls all weekend long from patients claiming to be some other physician's patient for whom I was covering on that particular weekend. Like all other residents, I would call in dozens of prescriptions for patients whom I would never see.

Such examples are only the tip of the iceberg. As a resident, I also admitted literally hundreds of patients to the hospital for private physicians. You know the routine: you are sick and your doctor tells you to go to the emergency room because his office is full and he can't see you now. You end up getting admitted to the hospital and some resident comes down, examines you, and takes your medical history. You then see your regular doctor the next day when he makes hospital rounds. But he never actually performs a physical examination.

Amazingly, many of the patients I admitted to the hospital had never seen their doctor in person before. Many patients, whether with chronic illnesses or no past illnesses at all, had personal physicians whom they had not even met. Many more patients had not seen their doctor in person for years—not months, but years. These people had been having prescriptions called in to their pharmacy for years without ever seeing their doctor.

There are many reasons for such understandable—but technically illegal—practices. Sometimes a doctor retires and another one takes over. Sometimes the doctor-patient relationship has been kindled for so many years that the physician just doesn't make the patient come in for annual visits. Sometimes the patient is involved with a large group of physicians and was originally assigned to a doctor who is no longer there. That patient now gets assigned to various other physicians in that same group but never really sees any of them. Sometimes the patient is encouraged to stay home because the physician doesn't like to see him or her in person. Annoying patients readily get their prescriptions called in so as to keep them out of the office. Also, people with chronic illnesses who are on lifelong prescription medications rarely see their doctors for prescription refills. The list of reasons could go on.

Physicians call in more prescriptions today than when I was a resident. Physicians now spend less time in their office and more time with their families, in meetings, vacationing, and so on. Because they are readily available by beeper and cell phone, it is much easier for physicians to get out of the office to do other things. Almost every physician in this country is prescribing medications to patients without ever seeing or examining them.

Let's go back to that examination physicians are supposed to do. What is an examination anyway? Is it simply taking a history, or are there definitive areas a physician must physically examine in order for the physician's actions to be considered an examination? Is the physician required to do weights, blood pressures, examination of the ears, nose, and throat, listening to the heart, lungs, and stomach, performing a rectal or pelvic examination? Must this occur every time medication for a chronic disease is prescribed or can there be exceptions when an examination is not necessary?

Finally, what is a dangerous medication? If any prescription medication is considered a dangerous medication, then examples would include antibiotics, inhalers, epinephrine pens, kwell shampoo, pyridium, birth control pills, steroids, and many more. According to the State Pharmacy Board, every time your doctor calls in a new prescription for you, whether it is for antibiotics, birth control pills, or acne medicine, he is breaking the law if he has not done a face-to-face evaluation and examination on you.

Physicians also call in prescriptions for obvious ailments without doing an examination. Examples abound. A friend from out of town is visiting and is normally on an inhaler for asthma. Or, a person tells the physician she is going camping and her son is deathly allergic to bee stings. In these two cases, most physicians would prescribe a new inhaler prescription for the asthmatic and an epinephrine pen for the family going camping—without ever seeing the patient or doing an examination. According to the agencies that want to put me in prison, that is illegal. And yet it is common practice.

This illegality includes the use of physician assistants (PAs), who help take care of emergencies. PAs often examine, treat, and discharge emergency room patients without the physician in charge and on record even seeing those patients. PAs tell the physician in charge what the patients are complaining of, what was found on examination, and what treatments are recommended. When the physician in charge is busy and the presentation by the PA is reasonable, the patient is discharged from the ER without ever being seen by the physician in charge. These patients receive signed prescriptions from emergency room physicians who never even laid eyes on these patients. These patients never saw anyone other than the physician assistant during their entire emergency room stay. That too is illegal according to the agencies after my freedom.

The point is that physicians are willing to treat obvious conditions without an examination or face-to-face visit. This is not a bad thing! No one follows the law and our patients thank us for that! Physicians do not prescribe medications when they don't know what is going on with a patient. I know for certain that many psychiatrists never do a physical examination and those who do physical examinations would never do more than one on the same patient! Psychiatrists are always calling in prescriptions for patients that they have not examined. They also call in prescriptions for patients with chronic psychiatric illnesses whom they do not see in their office.

Ironically, then, physicians oppose Internet medicine without realizing that they have been paving the way for the very type of practice they oppose.

Physicians detest being told how to do their jobs just as much as other professionals do. Physicians believe they, and not the government, have the right to decide when a face-to-face visit and examination are necessary to treat a particular patient. But most physicians could not survive if they had to examine or see every patient for whom they prescribe medications during the day and night. No physician would be willing to take call for another doctor if they were required to examine and see all of that other physician's patients while on call. Many specialists who are in hospitals doing procedures during the day and who only have office hours several times per week don't have time to see every patient before prescribing each patient's medication. To be precise, it usually isn't even the physician who calls in prescriptions for his patients, but a nurse. The bottom line here is that physicians do not and cannot see all of their patients before prescribing medications to them. Traditional physicians cannot support laws banning Internet physicians from treating patients simply on the claim that Internet physicians are not seeing or examining their patients. These laws would also have to apply to traditional physicians.

An easy way to enforce the law that physicians must see every patient, every time they prescribe, would be for physicians to be banned from calling in prescriptions. In other words, no patient would be allowed to get medication from the pharmacy without a written prescription, signed and handed over in person by a physician after his examination. As it stands, pharmacists never ask for proof that patients have actually been examined by their physicians prior to being allowed to have prescriptions filled.

Of course, state agencies don't really want to enforce this law on everyone. They just want it available to ruin the lives of those physicians they feel are a threat to their power and control.

I treat patients in a way that is new and different from the way many physicians currently practice medicine. Many people like my way better than they like the traditional way—the numbers do not lie. I have 150 new patients every week because so many people in this country prefer the convenience and privacy of Internet medicine.

I don't expect physicians to support Internet medicine, because I understand how threatening it is to their livelihoods. However, I do expect them as fellow physicians to stand up and support me against the state's charges of drug trafficking. Remember that the Ohio State Pharmacy Board is arguing that any physician who prescribes medication to a patient he has not seen is guilty of drug trafficking.

Internet medicine physicians are not any more guilty of drug trafficking than any other physician in this country!

Once, a traditional physician actually admitted to me that although all physicians do occasionally prescribe medications without seeing patients, Internet medicine should still be banned because the physician *never* sees them. He was arguing that not seeing patients before prescribing medications is all right on occasion. But a crime is still punishable, whether it is done once, daily, weekly, or annually. The bottom line is simple: physicians with traditional practices will never see and examine every patient before a prescription is written.

In fact, technology will soon enable Internet physicians to see *more* patients face-to-face than traditional physicians can. With the new teleconferencing technology that is currently available, it will not be long before all Internet patients are seen by a physician prior to receiving their medication. Even Kinkos now offers tele-conferencing for those who don't have computers. Computer video cameras already allow people who do have computers to talk to and see the person with whom they are communicating. The government plans to fund telemedicine projects for rural areas where physicians are scarce, a precedent that obviously opens up the way for allowing Internet medicine to serve patients far better than traditional medicine can.

Suppose you take medicine for high blood pressure and are out of your medication, but you don't have a physician because you moved from another city three months ago. You could call and make an appointment to see a new physician, but it could be three weeks before you can get in to see him or her. Another option would be to get on your computer (or go to Kinkos if you don't have a computer in your home or office) and see and talk to an Internet physician on duty. Internet medicine, by its very nature, will have 24-hour around-the-clock coverage 365 days per year. Your medication could be sent to your home or business the very next day if necessary. If pharmacies require written prescriptions, the Internet physician can electronically send you a prescription that has the physician's actual signature on it!

Traditional physicians will not be able to compete with Internet medicine whether the old law is enforced or not. However, traditional physicians will have less likelihood of surviving than Internet physicians will, if the rule requiring physicians to see every patient prior to prescribing medicine for them is actually fully enforced.

Finally, the minimum standard of care requirement is where the worst hypocrisy comes into play. A physician is considered negligent and incompetent—and sometimes guilty of malpractice—when he does not provide the minimum standard of care that a patient would have received from any other physician. Because of my Internet medicine practice, I am being accused of neglect and failing to provide the minimum standard of care for my Internet patients. Ironically, however, this could be said of *all* of Ohio's physicians who, because of Ohio's strict weight-loss rules, are prevented from providing the minimum standard of care to over 35% of all their patients. A physician who refuses to treat obesity falls short of this minimum standard. If you compare me with other Ohio physicians, then, I have *actually exceeded* my comrades' standard of care in treating the disease known as obesity.

The State Pharmacy Board needs to recognize that for

many chronic illnesses the minimum standard of care means not seeing or examining the patient afflicted with a chronic illness. The medication the physician provides the patient is the minimum standard of care. Patients will survive without an examination, but they need the medication! Smokers need Zyban to help them quit smoking. Patients with recurrent genital herpes need Valtrex to decrease their pain and suffering. Patients going bald need Propecia to help prevent further loss of hair. People with sexual dysfunction need Viagra™ to improve their sex lives. And, contrary to society's myths, obese patients need weight-loss medications.

Some people question the safety of getting treatment over the Internet. Or, from the doctor's perspective, another question arises: what if the patient is lying?

As for the danger of obtaining medication over the Internet, the actual medication patients would receive from their family doctors is exactly the same. A better question would be something like this: Is there anything my family doctor would be able to tell me about the medicine or anything that he would find in a face-to-face examination of me that would stop him from giving me the medication that I am seeking? If the answer to this question is yes, then the Internet physician should not be used to obtain that medication.

Ironically, however, in many instances the Internet may actually be *safer* for the patient than a visit to her regular physician. Often, the family physician is too busy to answer all of a patient's questions. At other times, the patient is too embarrassed or intimidated to ask the appropriate questions. Also, a patient who utilizes an Internet site has the ability to change his mind and cancel the entire consultation and treatment right in the middle of it!

Let me give you a real example of this scenario. A man with sexual dysfunction wants to try Viagra™ and makes an appointment with his doctor. Two weeks later, he misses several hours of work so that he can see his doctor. The doctor is behind schedule and the man has to wait an extra hour to be seen. The nurse raises her eyebrows when reading the patient's chart and the doctor finally sees him and writes him a prescription for Viagra™. He then goes to the pharmacy and pays several hundred dollars for his prescription, which takes another half an hour to get ready. The pharmacist then talks to him about the side effects of Viagra™ in front of several younger women also waiting in line. He finally gets home, five or more hours after leaving work for his appointment. At this point, what are the chances that this guy is now going to change his mind and reconsider taking Viagra™?

Now, suppose the same guy orders his medicine on the Internet after filling out a 10-minute medical history consultation just before going to bed one night. The next morning he decides to hold off on getting Viagra™ until it has been in use longer. He simply gets on the Internet and cancels his order and it is canceled!

From the doctor's perspective, there is also more opportunity to make sure the medicine is warranted. Obviously, the Internet physician must avoid treating patients who have medical conditions they are not aware of, conditions which contraindicate the medicine they desire. As stated earlier, this information is obtained from the patient's medical history, not from an examination—exactly the way the patient's regular doctor decides what treatment he should have!

Remember, a traditional physician cannot detect coronary artery disease or whether a patient is lying during a physical examination. Meeting a patient in person, the physician cannot determine whether those patients requesting Viagra™ really have sexual dysfunction or whether they are being dishonest simply to try out Viagra™. Patients can lie to a physician just as easily in person or on the Internet.

Let me give you another real example—one that may save someone's life! Several years ago, a 39-year-old female nurse with whom I was working started complaining of intermittent chest pain while working or exercising. She had several examinations, EKGs, blood work, and a stress test by a superior cardiologist. She continued to have intermittent chest pain that worsened until she had difficulty working. I told her to see the cardiologist again and ask for a heart catheterization to see if she had coronary artery disease. Her cardiologist had already told her to see a stomach doctor because he didn't think it was her heart. Two days later we visited her in the cardiac care unit, where she had been admitted after her heart cath showed blockage of all three of her coronary arteries! She later ended up having bypass surgery. Clearly, this woman had a much more thorough examination than anyone who wants Viagra™ is required to have; she even had numerous heart tests, which failed to detect her coronary disease. Her severe life-threatening heart disease was initially not detected through a physical examination by one of the best cardiologists in the USA.

In another case proving the futility of exams, a good friend of mine was prescribed Viagra™ by his physician even though he also takes isosorbide—a form of nitrate. His doctor saw him, examined him, and then almost killed him! The physician who saw him in person failed to protect him, even though Viagra™ is strictly contraindicated in any patient with heart disease or who is on nitrates such as isosorbide.

Some people will still argue that it is easier to lie to a physician on the Internet compared to face-to-face in a traditional practice. But people who are dishonest on the Internet can also be dishonest in the physician's office.

For this reason, I never offer narcotics on my Internet site. After all, no single, specific disease is treatable with narcotics. Physicians often have patients who want pain medications for various ailments including back pain and migraine headaches. Unfortunately, there is no method of determining when a patient is really having pain or simply wants pain medications. For this reason, I refuse to offer my Internet patients narcotics, which have a high risk for abuse in regular physician practices—a risk that would only be increased on the Internet.

News reporters, physicians, and pharmacists are quick to accuse Internet physicians of being nothing more than drug dealers. This is so ironic because the physicians with Internet practices in this country are very careful not to offer narcotics on their sites. Yet, sites from other countries often offer narcotics which can readily be ordered by U.S. citizens without even having to fill out a medical consult. Not to mention the fact that many traditional physicians write narcotic prescriptions for their patients on a daily basis. How many times have I heard about the narcotic addicts who have five or more family doctors in different parts of town who they visit to get their fix of pain medications? I have seen patients wanting pain shots in my emergency room who were found to have already received pain shots from at least two other emergency rooms that same day. The traditional physicians are the ones who write prescriptions for narcotics on a daily basis and yet the Internet physicians are the ones being accused of being the drug dealers.

People who lie in order to obtain prescription medications via the Internet should be held personally liable when they are caught. A person who gives false information about his weight so that he can get weight-loss medications should be held accountable for those actions. People should be prosecuted when caught telling lies to get prescription medications. But the unlikely possibility that someone might lie to receive expensive weight-loss medications with no street value can never compare to the actuality of the thousands of people who die every year of untreated obesity.

I prescribe two FDA-approved medications for weight loss: Phentermine and Meridia™ (both of which are less addictive than caffeine). Both are classified as class 4 medications because they are feared to be habit-forming. However, I have treated patients who said they took Phentermine for one to two years and had absolutely no withdrawal symptoms after stopping the medication. This certainly is not true with many nonprescription drugs such as caffeine, tobacco, and alcohol! Several thousand patients who took Phentermine administered by my own weight-loss centers confirmed how effective, safe, and non-addictive Phentermine is. Many other physicians have had the same success with Phentermine that I have experienced. Remember that anything you might have read about

Phentermine is from studies done 25 years ago. Furthermore, for obvious financial reasons no company that sells weight-loss medications will recommend Phentermine instead of their own weight-loss medications. I guarantee that Phentermine is a very safe and effective medication, but you won't read this safety analysis in any journal or in any study—because no one benefits from paying for such a study. Nevertheless, Phentermine can be used successfully for weight loss in over 90% of patients afflicted with obesity.

I honestly think we would be better off if we were too liberal with regards to the treatment of obesity, rather than too conservative. What I mean by this is that we should allow people to get their weight-loss medications at any grocery store without having to present a prescription for their medicine. The minimal risk involved is nothing compared to the benefits that millions of obese Americans would gain from having easy access to appropriate treatment for obesity.

I hope this book has demonstrated that I am not a drug trafficking, money laundering, racketeering physician. The medical profession simply does not know how to deal with Internet medicine, a serious threat to many physicians and pharmacists in this country. Internet medicine should be regulated, not banned. As it stands, some foreign-based websites allow U.S. citizens to order many medications from Europe without even filling out a medical history. I disagree with this practice. If Internet medicine is to be a safe, private, and convenient method for anyone to get medical care once they have a diagnosis, we must regulate what can be offered and make sure all the Internet sites are credible. Patients who choose to be treated on the Internet need to have their private medical histories kept private. They must be protected from scams. Their credit card information should be kept secure. Their medication should be exactly what they paid for.

But it will be very difficult to have legitimate Internet medicine sites available for people if agencies are threatening all such sites with felony charges. Internet medicine needs regulation, not banning!

I intend this book to be a call to action.

The Ohio State Medical Board will be having public hearings with regards to Internet medicine as early as this fall, but I don't recommend that you attend because the Board has already made up its mind to ban Internet medicine. There were public hearings for weight-loss rules as well and look how helpful they were! Other states will also be pushing to ban Internet medicine altogether.

Internet medicine allows many Americans the ability to choose a private and convenient method of treating certain known illnesses. I maintain that everyone should be able to choose whether to visit his or her physician in person or to visit a Cyber Doc on the Internet. Citizens should not allow any State Medical Board to take away that freedom to choose.

Tele-medicine is already being funded by government grants in many states, including Ohio. How ironic that the State Medical Boards want to ban something that is being promoted in their own states by government funds. Talk to your state representatives about your concerns with regards to banning Internet medicine.

If you like traditional medicine, like waiting for appointments, and like limited privacy—then do nothing. If you want the convenience and privacy of Internet medicine, then help fight for your right to choose!

I also expect Ohio physicians to atone for their disregard for their patients with obesity. Physicians have the power to abolish these weight-loss regulations that are such an embarrassment to our great state! Again, the media can be very helpful with regards to the practice of Internet medicine. The media has the ability to show people just how safe, convenient, and private Internet medicine really is. The media can show how worthless many of our doctor visits really are! Send news reporters into physicians' offices to obtain different medications. Interview patients going to the pharmacies to pick up their medications and ask them if they actually saw their doctor before getting their prescription filled. Also ask them if they had an examination by their doctor. Do stories on how tele-medicine is making medical care more convenient to those in rural areas where physicians are nonexistent. Interview Internet patients and have investigative reporters obtain these medications in both the traditional and Internet pathways so viewers can see firsthand the pros and cons of the two options. Newspeople know that there are two sides to every story. I have just given you enough information to change medicine back into an institution dedicated to serving people.

Physicians are not going to sit back and allow this book to be the last word with regards to Internet medicine or even obesity. They are going to put up a defense that will seem very credible on the surface. However, when the dust settles it will be obvious that the traditional medical community is very sick and a treatment has been developed which can prolong the life of medicine. There is no justification for the medical community's neglect of those suffering from obesity. There is also no justification for all Americans to allow such neglect to continue any longer! Internet medicine will survive the vicious attack by traditional medicine because people will demand Internet medicine. Everyone who has experienced the ease, convenience, and confidentiality of Internet medicine will be promoting its continued existence. It is clear to those who have already utilized Internet medicine that it is much better than traditional medicine for many treatments.

Even though obesity and Internet medicine would not be considered life-changing issues for most Americans, they will soon be household topics that are debated, rejected, defended, and scrutinized by politicians, lawyers, judges, talk shows, the news media, and governmental agencies throughout this country. I list obesity first out of respect for all of the years this serious disease has been ignored by America and out of respect and regret for all of those Americans afflicted with obesity who have suffered due to America's misunderstanding of this disease. I feel honored to be able to defend obesity and Internet medicine, yet surprised that these issues even need to be defended. These two issues affect every American, and yet only one side of this story has ever been presented to us.

The next time you see someone who is overweight, remember that obesity is even more dangerous than heart disease because it is not considered a disease at all by many Americans. Don't ever make fun of someone who is afflicted with obesity, any more than you would make fun of someone with cancer. And the next time someone tells you how dangerous it is to order medications over the Internet, tell them that they must be mistaken. Tell them that it is a safe, convenient, and far more private way of obtaining your treatment—as long as the patient already knows what is wrong with him.

It is the medical community that is looking for protection, not Americans. The real danger that comes from Internet medicine is that traditional medicine will become obsolete. I would like to think that Internet medicine is an adjunct to traditional medicine, something that will improve rather than destroy traditional medicine. But it will not be long before most people receive their medical treatment by computers and teleconferencing. Only a minority of patients will actually need to see a physician in his office. There will be an excess of physicians who will not be able to find work, except at much lower pay rates than they are used to living on. Physicians will only survive if they are good, have more flexible office hours, and have the ability to get along with their patients. Those physicians that think the world moves around them will never survive this weeding out process. Americans are ready for Internet medicine, even though the traditional medical community is not ready.

Internet medicine will survive because Americans don't like what has happened to medical care in this country. People don't like having to wait weeks or months for routine physician visits. People don't like missing work for routine physician visits and they really hate waiting several hours for office visits because the physician is overbooked or had to deal with some other emergency. Finally, people want more privacy for the treatment of some of their ailments then the traditional office visit can supply. There will be those physicians who will initially hate the idea of Internet medicine, only to change their mind after reviewing the facts. They will see how adding Internet medicine to their own practice would be a great benefit to many of their own patients. These physicians will see that Internet medicine doesn't have to be a threat.

PART THREE

Personal Skeletons, Views & Updates

THE FIRST TWO SECTIONS OF THIS BOOK WERE WRITTEN IN ORDER to acquaint Americans with the topics of obesity and Internet medicine. Specifically, the book raved about how unfair the medical community and its governing agencies have been with regards to these two topics. This final section will be more personal as I attempt to make myself more vulnerable. This is necessary because the easiest way to defeat an adversary is by destroying his credibility. This section starts with a brief description of what happened to my Internet medicine practice after the raid. Then I discuss some of the skeletons in my closet so that the opposition has less ammunition available to them when they attack my character. My personal views on issues not related to obesity or Internet medicine, are then discussed in brief detail. I have some skeletons in my personal closet that need to be exposed by me rather than by the media or some government agency. It is much better for people to find these things out from me, rather than from some outside source that could make these skeletons appear much worse. I will do this without fear of hurting any of those close to me because my friends already know that I have skeletons. To be honest, we all have some! I will also provide my own perspectives on law, divorce, taxes, sex, families, and business. After talking about skeletons and personal views, I will finish by discussing recent events with regards to obesity and Internet medicine that relate to this book and have occurred since I began writing this book only eight months ago. I hope that thus far, this book has been both enlightening as well as entertaining. Life is much too short for people not to see some of the humor along the way... no matter how tough our own travels have been. I also hope that this final section convinces you that I really do have some valid points with regards to Internet medicine and obesity. So valid, that no efforts should be made to have me imprisoned and to have my medical license taken away. Instead, efforts should be made to offer appropriate treatment for obesity throughout this country and additional efforts should be made to regulate rather than ban Internet medicine.

WHAT HAPPENED TO MY INTERNET MEDICINE PRACTICE AFTER THE RAID?

As you recall, I had the unpleasant experience of being visited by 10 unmarked cars at my place of business on Feb. 17th of 1999 and I now call that event the raid! These cars were filled with people carrying out a search warrant that accused us of possible drug trafficking, racketeering, and money laundering activities. The people instigating this raid were part of the State Pharmacy Board. They knew that I was doing Internet medicine and decided that the best way to deal with such a practice was to stop it by force and intimidation. Remember, that there are not now nor were there laws then against Internet medicine and I had spent thousands of dollars on legal counsel to make sure that Internet medicine was not illegal before our company even proceeded with Internet medicine. Our computers, patient records, files, ledgers, etc... were confiscated during this raid. We were told that we were not being arrested but that the evidence they had confiscated would be used to attempt to obtain an indictment against us by the Grand jury. I filed a civil suit against the State Medical and Pharmacy Boards in July of 1999 for one dollar! This suit was obviously not done for money. I did this because they are violating my rights to practice medicine and my rights to run a legitimate business. The Ohio weight-loss rules are immoral and violate my oath to treat disease. They have also taken away my patients' rights of patient- doctor confidentiality. Finally, they have also violated the patient's right to choose the type of medical treatment they want. Their response to this suit was swift. Indeed, I was indicted on July 9_{th} of 1999, less than one week after I filed suit, and charged with 64 counts of drug trafficking and selling of dangerous drugs. So, what happened to my Internet medicine practice? The day we were raided was the day we totally stopped filling any Internet prescriptions for Ohio residents. Did I stop practicing Internet medicine? No, yes and no! We continued to practice Internet medicine another several weeks for patients in all states except Ohio. Our Internet medicine practice was finally shut down completely for about one month when the Pharmacy Board froze our bank account and thus successfully stopped us from continuing with Internet medicine utilizing our original web sites. We had spent months and tens of thousands of dollars to make our web sites popular. At the time we were shut down, we were recognized as the Internet medicine leaders in most of the major search engines on the World Wide Web. We had also spent thousands in advertising in both National and local magazines and newspapers in order to become recognized as a legitimate Internet Medicine company. We were signing up over 200 new patients every week. We had over $55,000.00 in our company bank account that was spontaneously frozen and made unavailable to us when the Pharmacy Board had our account frozen. I had over 1500 Internet patients around the country that were lost to competitors because my Internet site could no longer remain operational. The State Pharmacy Board then had the audacity to contact my Internet patients and question them about their medical histories and treatments they had received from me, their physician. What ever happened to physician/patient confidentiality? According to these guys, when you meet your physician online, there is no such privacy. How ironic, since the reason many of my patients chose the Internet was because they had herpes or sexual dysfunction and wanted to keep these medical problems more private! Thus, about two weeks after the raid, we were put out of business. Our attorneys pointed out that it would probably cost over $100,000.00 to defend us if we were indicted & they wondered where I would get that kind of money. I decided that I would not give in to the pressure put on me to stop Internet medicine. My partner & I had a new Web site up and running, within 4 weeks of having our original sites shut down. We also had acquired a mail order pharmacy that would fill our patients prescriptions...since our application had already been refused. Our bank, pharmacy, and corporation were of course, started in a state other than Ohio. By the time our new web site was operational in April of 1999, we found ourselves engulfed in competition. There were many physicians now doing Internet Medicine & some International companies were doing Internet Medicine without even using a physician! I was amazed at how popular Internet medicine had become in less than 2 months. Thus, we started doing Internet Medicine in September of 1998 and have continued this practice with a brief break in March of 1999 while our new sites were being developed. I was indicted in early July of 1999 and I continued to practice Internet Medicine until October 1st of 1999. I stopped practicing Internet medicine on October 1st of 1999 after some new regulations went into effect in Ohio. During that year of practicing Internet medicine, thousands of patients around this country had obtained their prescriptions from me after I approved their medical consultations. These patients were treated for medical problems such as sexual dysfunction, baldness, obesity, acne, skin wrinkles, arthritis, and genital herpes. They received the same medications that their family doctor would have prescribed if they had chosen to see the family doctor rather than me. None of them were harmed or disappointed with the treatment that they received from me and all of them chose to be treated by me of their own free will. I am often asked why I didn't just stop doing Internet medicine after the raid. My answer is actually very practical. After being raided by the State pharmacy board, we asked our attorneys if they would just leave us alone if we stopped doing Internet medicine. We were told in no uncertain terms that even if we never did Internet again, they would not stop! They wanted to make an example of me! Now, add to this the fact that it was going to cost me over $100,000.00 for my defense (money I could not possibly have raised without doing Internet medicine) and you can understand how simple it was for me to continue with this practice. Finally, by quitting Internet medicine voluntarily, I would be admitting some kind of wrong-doing when Internet medicine is not illegal! I am not a felon and don't deserve the abuse I have received since starting my Internet medicine practice. I have spent most of my adult life utilizing my medical skills to serve those in need of medical assistance. What kind of thank-you is this? Stripping me of my medical license and putting me in prison for coming up with a safe, convenient, and private way to obtain medical care is not any way to thank me for improving medical care in this country. By the way, I didn't come up with the idea of Internet medicine, but I plan on taking the credit for defending it and making it common place in the near future!

My first web sites were www.get-it-on.com and www.cybrx.com. We decided to stop utilizing these two sites shortly after we were raided. We then started a new corporation called DVM enterprises and began a new web site at www.cybrxpress.com . When we first started doing Internet Medicine back in September of 1998 there were at least 8 other companies doing Internet Medicine in the USA and by the time we were raided in February of 1999 there were already over 50 companies competing with us for patients. At the time I was indicted in July of 1999, there were already several hundred Internet sites competing for patients. Shortly after my indictment, Kansas did a "sting" operation where they had people order medication from different web sites, followed by subpoenas and civil charges against those companies and physicians they had received medications from. About this same time, one of my clients turned out to be a reporter for US News & World Report that took it upon himself to help protect Americans from the atrocities of Internet medicine. It thus came as no surprise when his article mentioned our company in unglamorous terms. Thus, by summer of 1999, I had criminal charges in Ohio and civil charges in Kansas. I have given attorneys over $100,000.00 in retainer fees and they already want more! I now have another site up at www.rxclinic.com and plan on another site before this book is in print at www.eprescribe.com. I expect to recruit doctors throughout this country to help serve all of our new and existing patients. We plan on increasing our marketing campaign and eventually having the best Internet medicine practice in this country. It has come as no surprise to me that business is booming because Americans enjoy the freedom, convenience, and privacy of Internet medicine. Obviously, there are many people in this country that don't want to see me succeed with my plans. Instead, they want to take away my medical license, make Internet medicine illegal, and put me in jail. The Ohio State Medical Board is currently attempting to make me defend my Internet practice before their board members. Their ultimate goal is to suspend my Ohio medical license because of my unconventional practice. The State Pharmacy Board has gotten me indicted and forced me to defend myself in court. It is easy to see that I could be destroyed and imprisoned before this struggle is over. The question that you the reader have to ask yourself is this: Am I some crazy guy that couldn't possibly be on the right track with regards to obesity and Internet medicine? After all, how could all of those other people be so wrong and I be the only one that is right? How could the Government allow obesity to go untreated if it really kills 300,000 Americans annually? Wouldn't our government have already forced State Pharmacy & Medical Boards to allow physicians to adequately treat obesity? In fact, at a recent American Obesity Association conference in Washington, it was reported that healthcare costs for Obese adults in the USA in 1999 will be over 238 billion dollars…not million, but billion! Has our government ever made such a costly health related mistake in the past? Yes! Our government is currently involved in a huge civil lawsuit with the Tobacco Industry. The government is trying to recover billions of dollars spent in health care because of cigarettes. You see, the government is not always very quick in protecting the health of Americans. It is only now, after individuals have successfully won class action suits against the Tobacco Industry that the government is willing to go after the Tobacco Industry as well. Who should be sued for the billions we spend treating all of the medical problems caused by obesity such as heart disease, gallbladder disease, asthma, arthritis, cancer, etc…? Hmmm, probably all of those State Pharmacy and Medical Boards that prevent physicians from treating obesity appropriately. Also include those physicians that have failed to treat their own patients that are afflicted with obesity. I am sure the government will be happy to finish these guys off, just as the government is now happy to go after the Tobacco companies. My guess is that the government is not going to act until Americans take the first step. That first step will be class action suits that have been won by those Americans afflicted with obesity. These agencies and physicians have all been wrong with respect to obesity. They are also wrong with respect to Internet medicine because it is not bad for Americans! Internet medicine is only bad for the physicians that cannot compete with this type of practice!

This brings you up to date on what has happened to my Internet medicine practice since the raid. Before I discuss my skeletons, I would like to talk about how the Internet should be regulated.

REGULATING THE INTERNET

There are currently hundreds of Internet medicine sites available where patients can provide a medical online consultation and obtain treatment for various medical disorders by licensed physicians. Unfortunately for me, I am not allowed to practice Internet medicine myself because of the new Ohio regulations. Unfortunately for patients, many of these sites do not have conscientious physicians that will be taking care of them when they log on to those sites. Some of the International sites don't even have physicians. This brings me to the point where regulation must be discussed. Internet medicine needs to be regulated rather than banned. Does that regulation need to be done on a state by state basis or should it be a Federal issue? Actually, Ohio is not the only state that has filed legal actions against me. Several months after going online with our new sites, Kansas also filed civil suits against me. I expect that eventually all 50 states will want to take legal action against physicians for practicing Internet medicine in their state! Obviously, this should be a Federal and not a state by state issue because the Internet does not really lend itself to geographic restrictions such as state borders. Attorneys, realtors, stockbrokers, physicians, pharmacists, etc... no longer are simply practicing in their state of residence when they put their practice on the Internet. Suddenly, anyone in the world has access to someone's Internet practice. What is the difference between ordering something from California via the Internet and actually traveling to that same location in California and ordering something? Convenience and privacy are the only real differences between using the Internet and traveling somewhere in person. However, from a legal perspective, there is currently much more confusion with regards to the difference between the personal visit and the Internet visit. Is a California lawyer practicing law in Ohio or California when an Ohio resident consults him via the Internet? If the Ohio resident flies to his California office, we can say with confidence that the attorney is practicing in California. If the California lawyer flies to Ohio, we could say with confidence that he is practicing law in Ohio. When the Internet is used, both Ohio and California argue that the lawyer is practicing in their respective state. The Internet is changing the way we live. It may also change how we are licensed and regulated. Let me use a simple analogy using trains rather than the Internet. States don't have the right to make rules regarding the lengths of trains that pass through them because trains travel through all of the states in this country. If every state has a different train length that it allows, trains would have to stop before entering every state to adjust the number of cars it is allowed for that particular state. This would severely hamper the time it takes trains to make their destinations. Thus, states are not allowed to decide train length, it is a Federal issue. The Internet should also be regulated and it should be done on a Federal rather than a state by state level. **Internet medicine is not illegal in this country!** Well, right now it is still legal! Internet medicine is also unregulated in this country. As I predicted earlier in this book, many physicians, state agencies, and medical/pharmacy boards are trying their best to get Internet medicine banned. Why? Internet medicine is a serious threat to the type of medicine this country has put up with for so many years. Can you imagine how hard it is for your doctor to compete with a virtual medical clinic that is accessible from your own home 24 hours per day, 365 days per year! Not to mention the fact that there is also a virtual pharmacy available those same hours that can send your prescription to your home or office within 24 hours. This explains why physicians, pharmacists, and those associations related to them are threatened by Internet medicine. I honestly believe that the real issue, as far as government agencies are concerned, has nothing to do with being threatened and much more to do with control. I believe their motto is " if you cannot control it, ban it!" Internet medicine is a threat to traditional pharmacies and physicians because it offers convenience and privacy. Internet medicine is a threat to government agencies because they don't know how to control it! Some people have actually described the Internet as the "Wild West" because it is so unregulated. If you think about it, we didn't get to the 21st Century by banning new technologies and discarding new ideas. Instead, we grabbed on to the new ideas and technologies so that our lives could be better. Automobiles are a great advantage over horses but there are drawbacks. Thousands of people die and tens of thousands are injured every year in automobile accidents yet we will never ban automobiles. Instead, we make regulations that at least keep the deaths and injuries to a tolerable level. We accept the drawbacks because the benefits far outweigh them. I expect that the same thing will happen with Internet medicine because the benefits far outweigh the drawbacks.

My skeletons:

You can skip this section if you want! I wanted to give you a realistic picture of the kind of man that is writing this book. I thought there was no better way to know me then by learning about some of my skeletons and beliefs.

Divorce & kids:

I suppose I should talk about divorces & kids first. I started dating my childhood sweetheart when I was 12 and she was 15. I married her when I was 19 and she was 22. We had our first daughter five years later. After 9 years of marriage we divorced. Within 1 year we remarried and remained married another 9 years. We had two more daughters during that remarriage and we finally separated for good in 1991. What caused the breakup? Religion and growing apart were the main issues that caused our breakup. She became very involved with a local church and I eventually dropped out of that same church. I remained single after that divorce until

December of 1995 when I married a gal I had been talking to by phone for over three months. After only one date in person, we made arrangements to marry later that month in Vegas. The marriage was a disaster for both of us. The only good thing that happened was she got pregnant on our honeymoon and now has a healthy baby boy. I may not see my son until he is an adult, however, because there is still so much friction between his Mom and me. I have three daughters and a son… ages 20,14,12, & 3 at the time of this writing. I love my kids but have not been a good father. I could make excuses and blame others for my incompetence as a father… but I will not! As much as I would like to blame others, I must admit that I could have been much better with my kids.

Taxes:
Taxes should be discussed so that the facts are not confused at a later time! Until 1997, I always paid my taxes. During my divorce in 1997 & 1998, I was strapped for money and was unable to make child support, temporary support, attorney fees, and taxes. I was informed in no uncertain terms that I only had one choice! Don't pay my taxes. That is the advice my attorney gave me. You see, you go to jail if you don't pay temporary support or child support. You lose your attorneys if you don't pay them. Nothing happens if you don't pay your taxes… as long as you file your taxes and don't commit fraud. Shortly after my divorce, I met with a bankruptcy attorney to discuss options. I planned on filing for bankruptcy in January of 1999. However, my Internet Medicine practice started to bloom around that time and I began to think I could avoid bankruptcy all together or at

least file a chapter 13. The difference between filing chapter 7 and chapter 13 bankruptcies is that in a chapter 13 filing, you plan to pay back a percentage of all your debts whereas in a chapter 7 filing you don't pay back any of your debts. Taxes, however, are always owed and do not go away with either bankruptcy filing. Unfortunately, our business bank account was frozen in March of 1999 & legal fees went through the roof with the Internet indictment. Thus, I have filed but not paid any taxes for 1997, 1998, and the current year of 1999. The frozen assets, along with the current attorney fees, would more than have covered my tax debt for 1997 & 1998. Obviously, tax debt never goes away & I will end up paying the IRS for years to come! Fortunately, there is no debtor's prison for those that owe taxes as long as they do not commit fraud. I am certain that the prosecution would love to discredit me by pointing out that I have not even paid any taxes since 1996. However, I have filed every year and plan on making payments to repay these past taxes as soon as the IRS meets with me and we come up with a payment plan. You see, the IRS is not very fast in getting back to people that are behind in their payments. Finally, I have paid over one million in taxes prior to 1997 and really have not had anyway to pay my recent tax debts as well as pay my attorneys and child support/alimony payments.

Sex:
Sex…that issue can remain in my closet, except to note that I really enjoy it and I have not had sex with my patients! I also have never had sex with children or non-consenting adults.

Drugs:
I tried marihuana when I was a freshman in college and I did inhale! I didn't like it and have not used anything since except alcohol. I have never tried cocaine, crack, heroin, or acid.

Gambling:
Gambling should be discussed since I am always gambling. I love playing pool for money, betting on dice and cards in Vegas or betting on riverboats. I have lost a little more money gambling in my lifetime than I have won. I am not a gambling addict and it has never interfered with my ability to pay my other debts. Many of you may wonder how I can say that since I am considering bankruptcy! Remember that I have been through two divorces in less than seven years and they are the only reason I have considered bankruptcy. Anyone that has had even one divorce can understand what a financial burden divorce can be on the breadwinner of the family. My gambling debt would not even cover a small percentage of the money I pay annually in child support and alimony. Actually, I have paid more in alimony and child support payments than most people will ever make in their lifetime. Anyway, I am a gambler and make no apologies for this.

It should be apparent to you, the reader, that I have many faults. I could be accused of being a divorcee, tax evader, gambler, and poor father. I am certain that these faults would be used to discredit me if at all possible in the courtroom. After all, I am doing the same thing by trying to discredit those attacking me. The difference is that I am willing to admit my faults whereas my attackers deny they have any faults. The other difference is that I am willing to lose my career and my freedom to defend obesity and Internet medicine. The agencies attacking me are not taking any personal risk in this battle. I honestly believe that Internet medicine is safe, effective, convenient, private, and legal! I also believe that America is ready for it! I also believe that America deserves better treatment for those afflicted with obesity. I am ready to lose everything so that obesity and Internet medicine can be given the recognition they deserve. My hope is that many of you that read this book will decide to stand with me on these issues.

Doc's Views

I thought that you should hear some of my views, since you know about my skeletons. This section represents my views on several topics that many of you can also relate to because of your own personal experiences. I admit that these views are based on my own personal experiences and that others may not agree with my views. However, these issues will help you understand me much better and may at least swing some of your votes to my side with regards to Internet Medicine... anyway, that is certainly my hope in laying my views open to your dissection.

Divorce:

I believe that divorce is when common sense wins over hope. Divorce usually occurs because two people are unable to continue to play well together. There are innumerable reasons why this happens but the ultimate culprits are money, sex, religion, and personality. In this country, the big losers in divorce are the kids. I married at the age of 19 to a woman I had dated for 7 years. We were married for 18 years with a several month interlude dissolution half way through our marriage. We had thus spent 25 years of our lives as a couple, raising three children, and planning our future. When it was over, I was devastated beyond belief. In many ways it was worse than the death of a loved one because I still had to interact with someone that had broke my heart. Then come the attorneys. I warn all of the married bread -winners to be wary of how devastating a divorce will be to your life. On top of the emotional turmoil that you will be dealing with, there will be the unbelievable financial stress. When I got divorced, I had been living in a $140,000.00 four-bedroom house with a car, van, camper, dog, cat, and three children. I made almost $170,000.00 per year and was in debt up to my eyeballs. I had no equity in the house (two mortgages) and owed over $50,000.00 in credit card debt. I also was paying off both of our student loans. I also owed my family trust over $50,000.00 because of the way we had lived for the 18 years prior to our divorce. While I was going to college and medical school, my wife obtained two Master Degrees. We both went to school and sent our kids to sitters and Day Care Centers while getting our education. We drove nice vehicles and lived in nice places. Even though I made $170,000.00 per year, we usually had nothing left to put in our savings account after paying all of our bills at the end of the month. Then comes the divorce. I had to move out and find an apartment. She gets an attorney and I get one. The court immediately wants her to get temporary support so that she and the kids can continue to live as they are accustomed. Both of the attorneys want retainers. Where in the world does this money come from? Only the extremely rich can even afford a divorce! Well, when it was finally over, I was paying much more than I could possibly afford with my current job. I was living in a one bedroom unfurnished apartment and adding an additional $2,500.00 to my credit card debt every month because I could not make all of the payments with what I made. In this country, child support is not based on what you owe other people…only on what you make! In other words, if you make $1000.00 per month, there is a chart they use to determine how much child support you will pay. That chart is fair if you have no other debt obligations, but what if you end up with previous debt obligations? The court doesn't care if you normally pay out $900.00 in bills every month…even if these are bills that your whole family had incurred during the marriage. I was required to pay child support and alimony payments that exceeded my salary after making my monthly debt payments…those that were acquired during our 18 years of marriage. There is another catch for those of you that are thinking that you would just quit your job if they expected you to pay more than you even made! You cannot quit your job! The judge will put you in prison if you quit doing what you are trained to do in order to get out of paying your support payments. Well, after one year of severe depression and another $60,000.00 of credit card debt, I finally got additional jobs to help make my payments and keep me out of bankruptcy. I had a dear girl friend during that time that will always be my friend even though we broke up after several years of dating. We used to go through the local paper every day hoping to find that my ex-wife had filed for a marriage license. She had a boyfriend and my children had hinted that they were planning to marry. This would have great positive financial consequences for me because I was paying her $1,300.00 per month in alimony on top of the child support payments and I would be paying these payments for a total of 12 years unless she died, remarried, or cohabited with some other man. I bring this up to prevent any Americans going through a divorce from making the horrible mistake that I made with regards to alimony! After two years of going through our daily paper, we finally got the news that they were going to marry. The Monday following their marriage I gleefully called the support office to inform them that I would no longer have to pay alimony because my ex-wife had remarried on the previous weekend. Several days later, the support agency called me back to inform me that I must continue to pay alimony because my divorce decree said nothing about having alimony stop if she marries again. I explained that I had a copy of the decree in front of me & it specifically stated that alimony stops if she cohabits, dies, or remarries. I also pointed out that alimony always stops when they remarry…Wrong! Unless your divorce decree specifies that alimony stops with remarriage, it will not stop. Well, in my case, my ex-wife's attorney deleted the line talking about remarriage and alimony! My attorney did not catch the deletion. My ex-wife still gets alimony until 2002 even though she has been married now for over 4 years! I even tried to sue my own attorney for malpractice when I discovered his mistake. I learned from that fiasco that attorneys stick together and rarely take such cases. Oh, I forgot to tell you why we got divorced in the first place. It was because I was not religious enough. I have to admit that this was the closest I have ever come to wanting to kill someone! I really do understand why so many homicides occur between couples going through divorce. I am not proud of admitting it, but I really wanted to kill my ex-wife the day I was informed that alimony would not stop. It is a good thing I didn't kill her because she has been a good Mother to my children and she wasn't worth going to prison for anyway! Now, I said I would not make any excuses for my failure as a Father to my children…but this alimony thing really did make it impossible for me to go to her house to see my kids for several years. It was simply too painful for me to see or communicate with the woman that had caused me such pain. By the way, you don't have to be a man to get the shaft with regards to divorce! I knew a female nurse that was working at least 70 hours every week to help pay the bills. She and her husband both worked and had one child. Her husband then lost his job and started staying home and playing Mr. Mom. When they got divorced, the judge told her that she must continue to work 70 hours per week because she is the breadwinner in that family. She had to pay him support payments and suffered greatly because of the divorce. I have another very good friend that was married for 7 years and had two children that can attest to how unfair divorce is for the breadwinner of the family. His wife made $10/hour when he met her & he made about $140,000.00 per year. After 7 years of marriage they got divorced. Within two years of the divorce he has already considered bankruptcy and now works 70 hours per week in order to survive…not to get ahead! On the other hand, his ex-wife now lives in a $175,000.00 home and gets over $3,000.00 per month in support. Beware to the breadwinner! I can warn people without ever expecting they will ever listen. I didn't listen myself! I remarried at the end of 1995 and was separated within 3 months. I was finally divorced in June of 1998 & visiting a bankruptcy attorney in September of 1998. I have a very good friend (another nurse) that continually reminds me how "stupid" I was to get married again! Well, I am now engaged to a wonderful woman that I will marry after this nightmare with those opposed to Internet Medicine has been put to rest. This time, I may let her be the bread-winner!

LAW
The Law in this country- my view!

I am involved in a type of medical practice that I refer to as Internet medicine. I started this practice only after high paid attorneys researched this type of practice and assured me that it was legal! My biggest crime prior to starting this practice was speeding! I had received no more than four speeding tickets in my entire life! Thus, I was horrified when I heard on my local TV station that I had been indicted by Ohio's Grand Jury this last summer. How could this happen to such a nice guy? Seriously, I could not understand why Ohio wanted me taken out of society and put behind prison bars? I am not a danger to you, the reader, or to my patients. Obviously, I am a huge threat to someone! Who? Well, I suppose that would be those people wanting Internet medicine banned! Hmmm...it seems my practice threatens all of those physicians that make their patients sit in their waiting rooms and wait to be seen! When is the last time you visited a doctor for a scheduled appointment and your doctor was not late? It has gotten so bad that you are actually happy if your doctor is only 30-40 minutes behind schedule! Let's get back to my view of the law in this country. I am sure that you have heard the saying " people that live in glass houses should not throw stones". Anyone reading this book ever smoke marijuana? Anyone reading that is under 21 years old ever drink alcohol or smoke cigarettes? How about driving your car while under the influence? The penalty for breaking any of these laws if you get caught is actually fairly minor when you look at the big picture. It may cost you several thousand dollars in attorney fees, several days in jail, and fines of several hundred dollars in the worst scenarios. Now compare that with what is happening to me for practicing Internet medicine… something that isn't even against the law! I have spent over $100,000.00 already in attorney fees. I have had my reputation in my community destroyed. I now face possible prison time and the permanent loss of my medical license, a license I spent two thirds of my life striving to obtain. This is not right! This is not what America law is all about. Sure, I have the right to fight accusations made against me… as long as I have money to pay the quality of lawyers I need to defend myself. I know that even if I win the court battles, I can't win back my career & the credibility where I live. My Internet competition is growing stronger while I grow weaker because of these allegations made against me. Why am I the only physician facing criminal charges when there are many other physicians practicing Internet medicine? I believe that I know the answer to this question. It is much less expensive for agencies to go after one physician than after many! Besides, if it can be made a precedent in one state that Internet medicine is now illegal… that case can easily be used to force all of the other physicians in all of the other states to quit practicing

Internet medicine. That is the upside for the agencies wanting Internet medicine banned. Of course, the down side can also occur! When I win this case in court, Internet medicine will flourish overnight! I have a little company but there are some huge multi-billion dollar companies out there. These companies can incorporate Internet medicine into their structure overnight because they have the physicians and pharmacies in place already. Once these companies are involved, there will be no way to stop Internet medicine from becoming as commonplace as the automobile. The agencies that want Internet medicine banned could be tied up in courts for years fighting the attorneys hired by these powerful multi-billion dollar companies, once they get involved with Internet medicine.

I believe that I have been singled out because I appeared to be an easy physician to defeat in a courtroom. I assure you that appearances are not always what they seem and that in this particular instance, those that want Internet medicine banned have chosen the wrong man to attack. I will win this legal battle and big business will shortly thereafter take over the practice of Internet medicine. Americans will also win because they will definitely benefit the most from Internet medicine. When this is all done, I think I may go back to South Dakota and Minnesota and get back into fishing, hunting, and golf again. Who knows, maybe I'll even start up some sort of Internet business that is less controversial! Even though I feel certain about winning the legal battles ahead of me, I know that my credibility will be attacked at every turn. Thus, I need to open my closet and pull out those skeletons that will be used to attack my credibility. I assume that everyone reading this book understands that the easiest way to defeat your adversary is by showing that they are not credible. If someone can be shown to be a chronic liar, for example, it is unlikely that anyone will ever believe them when they are in fact telling the truth. Well, I am not a liar but I do have some other faults.

I have unfortunately, gotten more personal experience with the law than I would have liked! I believe that the laws we have are meant to protect Americans. I also believe those laws are sometimes misused by individuals to destroy rather than protect people. For instance, we now have a law that requires the police to incarcerate any male accused of physically abusing his wife. This law, of course, was designed to protect spouses that are abused by their husbands and yet, not believed by the police that are called to the scene. We have all heard stories of women that were maimed or killed by their husbands shortly after the police had left the scene… not believing the woman's story. However, what prevents an angry spouse from getting her husband arrested, even though he really didn't do anything to her? I have had two close friends find themselves in jail because their wives accused them of assault when they had not even touched their wife. Let us talk about drug dealers for a minute. How does the law help us catch them? The goal is to catch the person that provides the drugs to the drug dealer, the drug dealer themselves, and the people that buy the drugs from the drug dealer. There are laws against possessing, selling, or using illegal drugs. There are also laws that allow enforcement agencies to seize property, assets, drugs, etc… if they can link these things to the illegal activities taking place. Like wives, can't government agencies also abuse the laws? Now, suppose that you have a legitimate business that sells herbal products to customers throughout the country and this business is definitely not a drug dealing business like the ones our laws our designed to fight. Unfortunately for you, someone starts the rumor that you are a drug dealer & that rumor is brought to the attention of the authorities. The authorities then get a search warrant to check out your operation. In this search warrant they accuse you of possible drug trafficking and the judge now gives them the authority to do much more than simply check out your operation. They have the right to seize your equipment, your business property, your bank accounts, and even your personal property & bank accounts. They can do this without ever having a trial or ever indicting you! You could then spend the rest of your life in court trying to get these things back even though you had a legitimate business. Your reputation, of course, would be ruined because all of the local news stations would be talking about the possible drug bust at your plant. Undoubtedly, your picture would be on television and in the paper for weeks after the search warrant was carried out…I know this from personal experience! All of this could happen without you ever being indicted, arrested, or even charged with any crime. Sound absurd? It is true! My business went through this very process except that I have also been indicted. I have been charged with selling dangerous drugs at retail and drug trafficking. This is ridiculous, of course, since I am a board certified physician that has been using FDA approved medications to treat my patients that have known medical ailments. But, suppose I really was a drug dealer. Why would these agencies ignore my supplier and my buyers? I will tell you why they are ignored! These agencies know that I buy my medications from reputable wholesale pharmaceutical companies that are very powerful and that would crush them in court. My buyers are also reputable individuals. Many of them are high- powered businessmen, physicians, attorneys, and professors. Some of them are in politics and others are spouses of those individuals I have just described. I am not a drug dealer. If I were a drug dealer, my supplier and my buyers would also be in serious trouble. After all, everyone buying my drugs knew that I was treating them on the Internet. If it is illegal for me to provide medications on the Internet, isn't it also illegal for someone to obtain them via the Internet. You could always argue that the buyers didn't know it was illegal to get medication from me! I certainly didn't know that it was illegal! Why? Because there are no laws against Internet medicine! I think the seizure laws also should be changed so that others don't suffer the abuse that agencies render when search warrants allow these agencies such power! No one should be able to seize assets simply because they have a search warrant! In America, you are supposed to be innocent until proven guilty!

If a physician is accused of malpractice in this country, there is a trial to determine if he is guilty or innocent. The trial is by the way, a civil trial…not a criminal trial. Even if the physician loses the trial, he does not face a prison sentence, but rather, he will face financial penalties. Malpractice can only occur if the physician meets very specific criteria. In other words, a physician is not guilty of malpractice simply because he did something wrong, that other physicians with the same expertise would not have done. The physician also has to cause harm to the patient because of his mistake that would not have occurred if the physician had followed the correct procedure. For instance, if a physician botches a procedure in someone that caused that patient's death, he is guilty of malpractice if that patient would have lived if the procedure was done correctly. However, if that patient's death would have occurred anyway, it is not malpractice. The man who suffers severe mortal internal injuries because his parachute doesn't open, is going to die whether or not any one procedure is botched or not. The otherwise healthy young man with meningitis will only die if his doctor misses the diagnosis and does not give him antibiotics quickly enough!

Now that you understand malpractice, where does my Internet Medicine practice fit into this picture? These patients already have their diagnosis, and the medications that they are prescribed are FDA approved for treating their particular ailments. In other words, your family doctor will use the same medications that I use to treat your illness. The difference is that they will make you come into their office on their terms and at their convenience, so that you can get a prescription from them ...even though you already know what is wrong with you! They will then make you go to a pharmacy in order to get your prescription filled. This process is not very private or confidential. It is inconvenient to say the least. Thousands of patients around this country are utilizing the Internet to obtain medical consultations and prescription medications. They are not in any danger, unless they are dishonest when giving their medical history or if they are on a foreign Internet site that does not even require a medical consultation. Do you think the reason that Internet medicine is being attacked is because patients are complaining? Of course not! That is not the case. The reason Internet medicine has come under attack has nothing to do with malpractice! Internet medicine has simply exposed many of the obsolete rules that are still officially on the books, even though physicians have not followed these rules for many years. Those that oppose Internet medicine want to put me in jail because I do not physically see the patients that I treat on the Internet. Also, I do not do a physical examination on them. The rules requiring a physician to see and examine every patient are obsolete! There would not be any physicians left in this country if all physicians had to follow these rules. Every physician has written prescriptions or had them called in for patients that they did not see or examine. We are taught to do this during our internship when we are responsible for hundreds of patients when we take call. Throughout our careers we become even better at making our diagnosis from the medical history and treating our patients with prescription medications without ever examining or seeing them! I have already given you most of my views on the laws so will keep this brief. Laws were made to protect Americans and improve our lives. As technology changes so do the laws. The Internet has made it possible for Americans to have convenient, private, and safe medical treatment for common ailments that are treated similarly throughout the world. Old laws that are not even enforced to regulate traditional medical practices cannot be used to ban Internet medicine. New laws need to be used to regulate Internet medicine so that it continues to be a safe, reliable, private, and convenient alternative for those Americans suffering from common ailments. These new laws will protect Americans rather than protecting those agencies that are so threatened by Internet medicine.

Unfortunately, it is very expensive to be vindicated by the law in this country and it is fairly safe to say that many innocent people are incarcerated in this country because they don't have the money to defend themselves.

Gambling

How many of you actually know much about how gambling was introduced into America? Many of you are probably opposed to gambling. I personally think that it is no better or no worse than any hobby and that even those that oppose gambling probably do it themselves in one way or another. Like any hobby, some people will become obsessed with it & those that oppose gambling would say that it is addictive and ruins many lives. Come on people, the same can be said for almost anything can't it? Some people are so addicted to work and the pursuit of money that they also ruin their lives. Other people get so addicted to one sport or another, that nothing else matters. Sure, some are lucky enough with their addiction to be recognized as sports stars, entertainers, or successful businessmen and they actually make their living entertaining others with their own addiction. But for many others, there is no fame or glory. For every pro golfer that is recognized as a superstar, there are thousands that also spend most of their life playing the game without ever getting paid or being recognized. The same goes for musicians, pool players, runners, singers, dancers, etc… The bottom line is that many people are so obsessed with a hobby that the rest of their life suffers because of it! Now back to gambling! Did you know that our first militia was formed because of the money raised from gambling? It was called the lottery & is still popular today. Ohio opposes gambling yet is very big in supporting its lottery! Many churches oppose gambling yet they have weekly bingo nights and even gambling nights to raise money for their respective churches. Many people throw in several dollars every week for sports pools for weekend football, basketball, or baseball games. Then there are the legitimate horse and dog races that occur in many of those states that supposedly oppose gambling. Now lets talk about casinos. You used to have to go to Las Vegas or Atlantic City in order to gamble in an actual casino. However, along came Riverboat casinos and Indian Reservation casinos to make it much easier to gamble in an actual casino much closer to your home. It is now possible to enter virtual casinos on the Internet as well, so that you don't even have to leave your home or office. Yet, many states still hold on to the myth that they do not and will not allow legalized gambling in their states. Historians will mock these hypocritical views with regards to gambling.

SEX

Sex is a big issue today and everyone has a view on it. My view is that sex between two consenting adults is all right. In fact, I don't think it is bad if more than two consenting adults are involved. I think prostitution should be legalized and regulated so that it is no longer controlled by the underworld. I think protection should be emphasized so that sexually transmitted diseases can be controlled. Ones sexual preference should not be grounds for whether or not they are hired, fired, promoted or demoted. It has become obvious that heterosexual relationships are not necessarily any more stable than homosexual relationships. Again, how ironic that many churches are strictly against homosexuality and yet, these same churches have many leaders which are gay! I for one would much rather go to a prostitute if it is legal, for sexual gratification, than to go to a bar and try to pick someone up for a one-night stand. The prostitute will not be offended when I leave, while the woman I have the one-night stand with may be very hurt! Except Nevada, prostitution is illegal in other states as far as I know. However, look in most local papers & yellow pages and you will find a large number of massager and escort services available! They are not all prostitutes but I guarantee you that some of them are! The last thing I want to talk about with regards to sex has to do with sexual dysfunction. Many men and women that were able to perform quite well sexually when they were younger, find that they are having problems attaining or maintaining erections, or achieving orgasm as they get older. There are medications now available that can help those of you that have such problems. You should look into trying one of these medications to see if your sexual dysfunction can be alleviated with one of these medications…once a doctor, always a doctor.

EMERGENCY ROOM MEDICINE

I have a view with regards to Emergency Room Medicine or ER Medicine for short because I was an ER physician for 12 years. The ER has become the dumping ground for those patients that no one else wants to treat. Part of the reason this has happened is because the ER fills such a vital function in the medical community. That function is to care for those patients that have a true medical emergency…the reason we call them emergency rooms in the first place!

Examples abound and include heart attacks, strokes, traumas, shooting victims, stabbing victims, overdoses, etc... However, most of the patients that are seen in an emergency room are not really emergencies at all! Instead, they are people with chronic or minor ailments that are visiting the emergency room because they don't have a doctor, their doctor is unavailable, or because their doctor is available but does not want to see them. The ER is not allowed to turn away a patient no matter what the complaint may be! You want examples? Doctor, I have had this lump for 2 years, I have had this stomach ache for 10 minutes, my back hurts when I stand all day, my throat itches, my skin is turning blue, my hands hurt when I type, etc... Most of the people seen in an ER could just as easily be seen at a later date in someone's office. The ER is open 24 hours every day, including holidays. Thus, many patients that have family doctors end up going to these ER's at night, on weekends, and on holidays. Here comes the scary part concerning ERs. **The ER is also the dumping ground for bad doctors!** ERs need physicians to work all of those shifts that exist when an ER department is open 24 hours every day. Most ERs are so busy that they require at least 6 doctors daily to supply adequate physician coverage. Unfortunately there are not that many good physicians available for most ER departments. Thus almost every ER ends up with some doctors that are only working there because of a lack of more qualified physicians to take there place. As sad as this sounds, and as wrong as it sounds, it is true! I have worked with physicians that were so incompetent that the nursing staff would draw straws to see who had to work with them. People died when these physicians were on duty that would not have died if a competent doctor had been on duty. You might think that I would be afraid to admit this fact! Well, I am not afraid to admit it because I can give numerous examples of actual cases that would prove that what I am saying is true! There are nurses that would substantiate that I am telling the truth. Do you know what happens when a bad ER physician is finally dismissed from an ER department? They end up working nearby in another ER department! This is really true. Bad ER physicians don't quit, they just move around more! Let me give you some examples of how bad it is in some ER departments. There was an ER doctor that did not realize his patient was having a heart attack even though the patient complained of chest pain and had an EKG that showed that he was having an acute heart attack. In the old days, doctors had to actually read an EKG and make his own interpretation of it. Today, the EKG also gives you a computerized interpretation and printout of the test. Not only was this physician's patient having an acute heart attack, but the EKG even came back with a printout that said he was having an acute heart attack! When the doctor was asked what he thought about the EKG and the computerized interpretation printed out on the top of it, he responded with the simple statement: "I don't believe the computer's interpretation." That doctor now works in another ER not far from the one where he missed the diagnosis of an acute heart attack! There was another ER doctor that would hide when it got busy in the department! The ER would have 20 new patients waiting to be seen and no one could find him. You think I am kidding? That ER doctor still works in several ER departments nearby. There are some excellent ER physicians in this country and they do not need to be defended. These excellent physicians are well recognized by their ER staffs. There are also some horrible physicians that work in these same ER departments…they are also recognized by their ER staffs. I loved working in the ER & I was very good at it. I have many friends that are ER physicians that are also very good. I also know ER physicians that are so bad that I wouldn't even let them see my neighbor's pet! This may all come as a shock to you the reader, but I assure it is not news to those hospital administrators that deal with their ER department. Why do you think the ER staff, hospital administrators, and their family members call ahead to see what ER physician is on duty when they have an emergency? In some hospitals, the emergency room is so understaffed that these hospitals don't even use emergency room trained physicians for backup when they get busy. They have physicians with absolutely no emergency room training come in to help out when the emergency room gets busy! The next time you are in a busy emergency room, ask the physician taking care of you what kind of emergency room training he has undergone. If you are not happy with the response, request a more qualified physician. How can we increase the number of qualified ER physicians so that the bad ER physicians can be replaced? Internet medicine may actually help make this possible because there will be less demand for traditional office based physicians once Internet medicine becomes more popular. There should then be more physicians available for real emergencies and less need for the office-based physician. The office-based physician usually spends most of his time treating routine problems that are just as easily taken care of by technicians, nurse practitioners, physician assistants, and Internet medicine practitioners. You may find it difficult to believe my last statement and certainly no office-based traditional physician will agree with me. However, if you ask the charge nurses, technicians, physician assistants, and nurse practitioners…they will agree with me entirely. Of course, they will only do this anonymously because they don't want to lose their jobs.

THE FAMILY DOCTOR

I also feel qualified to give you my view on the family doctor because I have seen all of his patients when they got sick at night, on weekends, and on holidays. Today's family doctor is as interested in his free time, family, and hobbies as he is in his patient's health. He or she has a real life outside of the office and is doing everything possible to have as much free time away from the office as possible. Life seems to center around the doctor and their attempts to have more free time. Your family doctor is facing a very tough dilemma. They are working harder to make less money. They want more free time but need to see more people in order to make enough money to enjoy there free time. Thus, your doctor now sees more patients per hour in order to have time off and enough money to enjoy that time off. They use pagers, beepers, cell phones, and faxes to communicate with patients and staff when they are not in the office. They don't have time in there busy schedule to see those patients that become sick and don't have appointments already scheduled. These "emergencies" are sent to the ER for someone else to deal with. They are busy seeing well people with no complaints or people with chronic illnesses that need medication refills. They share weekend and holiday call with other physicians so that the weekend or holiday you are on call…you are covering hundreds of patients that really belong to 5-8 other doctors. Thus the weekend or holiday that you are on call…you work very hard. On the other hand, you are free during the weekends and holidays that others are taking call. How is it possible to take call for all of those physicians when that also means you are covering for hundreds of patients that you don't know? Easy! Send the sick ones to the ER for them to deal with. Also send any of them that call you at inconvenient times, like bedtime, to the ER as well. Many of them you can talk to by phone and actually make a good guess as to what is wrong with them. You then call them in a prescription and tell them to make sure and follow up with there regular doctor the next week for a follow up visit to make sure they are getting better. Tell them if they are not getting better, to go to the ER for further assistance! Many doctors that take call manage to take in weekend activities such as sporting events, movies, golfing, tennis, dinning out, etc…while they are cross covering for their fellow physicians. The reason they can do this is because they don't actually see many of the patients that they treat! They talk with them on the phone and then make medical decisions about what should be done next with that patient. There is no face to face encounter and no physical examination. The difference between this and Internet medicine is that the family doctor on call is dealing with patients that don't even know what is wrong with them! The Internet medicine patient already knows what is wrong with them and is simply trying to obtain the FDA approved prescription for their known ailment. Internet medicine does not deal with emergencies whereas the doctor on call is often dealing with emergencies. Yet, the doctor on call gets in no trouble for prescribing medications and making diagnoses on the phone without ever seeing or examining their on call patients.

THE INDICTMENT

I have been charged with 64 counts of drug trafficking and selling dangerous medications. The number of counts is in itself of much interest to me as the actual charges, since I actually had over 1,000 patients at the time they did their raid and many of these patients had received at least two refills on their prescription from me. Why only 64 counts, when they have records that show I had done over 3,000 prescriptions at the time of the raid? I have been told by some attorneys (anonymous of course) that they want to punish me for practicing Internet medicine and they also would like to be rewarded financially if they win the case. The more counts of drug trafficking and selling drugs, the more punishment and the more financial gain...right? Not really! Actually, the more ridiculous their accusations become if they have too many counts and the more patients become available for me that can testify about the safety, convenience, and privacy of Internet medicine. Not to mention the fact that most of my patients are well respected in their own communities and could easily sway the jury to side with me if they were allowed to testify. My view is that the Grand Jury was misled into believing that these charges were plausible by a misinformed prosecuting attorney that relied on the biased opinions of the State Pharmacy Board. These are the same people that convinced the judge that a search warrant was needed because we were supposedly involved in drug trafficking, money laundering, and racketeering! They somehow even convinced the Grand Jury that I am not really a practitioner or physician even though I am licensed as a physician in Ohio. They also convinced the Grand Jury that I was selling dangerous drugs on a retail basis. Let me assure you that I am now convinced that you can get a ham sandwich indicted! I am now obligated into paying attorneys huge sums of money to show a jury what? My attorneys must prove to the jury that I am really a physician and that I don't sell dangerous drugs on a retail basis. Certainly, my current medical license is enough to validate that I am really a physician. And when is the last time you had to fill out a consult and be approved by a physician in order to buy your groceries or over-the-counter medications? In a nutshell, they convinced the Grand Jury that anyone that wants medications on my Internet site is allowed to get them as long as they pay for them. That would be true if they didn't have to fill out a medical consult that is reviewed and approved or rejected by a physician! The bottom line with regards to me being a practitioner is that the State Pharmacy Board has independently decided that a physician practicing Internet medicine is not really a physician! It is amazing how influential the State Pharmacy Board must be in order to get away with these ridiculous charges and assumptions that have no basis whatsoever! This is humorous from a law perspective …unless you are the one being indicted. Since, according to the State Pharmacy Board, I am really not a physician, they feel free to harass all of my patients and not give any credence to patient- physician confidentiality. I am a physician that is being abused, accused, and outright persecuted by those that oppose Internet medicine. My rights and the rights of all of my patients are being violated and there doesn't seem to be anything that I can do about it! Some day, someone is going to review all of the atrocities that my partner and I have had to endure while fighting against those Americans opposed to Internet medicine...they will be amazed that such atrocities were allowed.

BUSINESS

I run a business that is certainly not conventional. I like business and believe that in America people have great opportunities to succeed in business ventures. I wonder if the founders of Microsoft, Amizon.com, Ebay, etc... ever had to go through the kind of stress & roadblocks that we have faced in our Internet medicine business? You see, no matter what anyone says to you, medical practices are businesses! Hospitals that don't make a profit disappear. Private practices and group practices that fail to make a profit also disappear. My Internet business had its assets seized and or frozen within the first several months of operation. We have had criminal and civil charges against us in several states. Our patients are stripped of their civil rights for patient-doctor confidentiality. Government agencies have been caught declaring to our vendors that we are involved in illegal activity, even though there a no laws against Internet Medicine. We have a business that is very profitable to the attorneys that we retain and to the agencies that seize our assets. From a business perspective, Internet medicine could be made into a multibillion-dollar business overnight because there is a huge demand for this business in America. You may think I am exaggerating but it is true!

With less than $30,000.00 in marketing, we are going to break 5 million in annual sales for our first year! Imagine this type of success, even with all of the roadblocks that we have encountered. One of the biggest headaches in our business has to do with merchant services because our patients pay us with their credit cards. According to merchant services, new companies are not supposed to do over $50,000.00 per week in credit card sales. Because of this, our accounts are quickly flagged and money is often frozen for weeks. Thus, we often have problems paying our staff and vendors even though we have generated more than enough money to pay them…if it just wasn't frozen. We even had one vendor that called the DEA (Drug Enforcement Agency) to ask if we were doing anything illegal & of course, they were told to immediately freeze our money! Our money was later released after everyone realized that Internet medicine is not really illegal. Someday, I'll look back at all of this and laugh about my experiences in the Internet medicine business! Most businesses rely on marketing to get their business. When I first started doing Internet medicine back in September of 1998, I was advertising in magazines, newspapers, radio, and even television. Within months of getting the word out, my company was raided and my equipment confiscated. My assets were frozen and my business was basically shut down temporarily. I think that it is safe to say that the Internet business is a little tougher than most! I now laugh when I read about those opposed to Internet medicine because they are always pointing out that the companies that practice Internet medicine do not give out their addresses or phone numbers. They argue that these companies must not be legitimate because you can only reach them by email or fax. Actually, most of these Internet companies are legitimate and simply don't want to get raided by an over zealous State Pharmacy Board like I was! I actually understand from my own experiences why they need to do this and don't blame them one bit.

Children on the Internet

I have noticed that whenever Americans want to get something banned, they cry out "We need to protect our children from this!" The Internet has allowed kids and adults to access issues that normally would be more segregated. The Internet allows children to access many adult sites that were never intended to be accessible to children. Eventually, we will come up with methods of preventing kids from accessing adult sites so that parents don't have to baby sit their kids every time the children access the Internet. Many adult sites already have protective locks which deny anyone access without providing a proof that they are an adult. There are actual companies out there that charge people an annual fee to obtain an adult Internet ID. You are required to send in information that is verified before you get your ID. You then must use your credit card to pay the company and receive your ID. Unfortunately, many sites do not have such gatekeepers in place and thus children can often access many adult sites. I am often asked what prevents children from accessing my Internet medicine sites and I tell them that it will never be a problem. Why? First of all, the child would have to obtain their parent's credit card in order to attempt to obtain medications on my sites. Secondly, the medications we offer have no street value or recreational value for kids. Thirdly, these medications are expensive enough to deter even the most curious teenager from wanting to order them. Fourth, these medications are sent by Fed Express or UPS to the persons home or work place. This makes it very difficult for the child to receive the medication because adults typically accept such packages. Fifth, the child would easily be caught by the parent or credit card owner because of the easily followed tracking system which utilizes the credit card itself, the actual shipping address, the filled out medical consult, and the UPS or Fed Express tracking system which verifies where the package went. Finally, the medications used are not anymore dangerous to children than most over the counter medications. Children are not going to obtain prescription medications over the Internet that have no recreational value and that cost over $150.00 when they have much easier access to street drugs that cost far less. It is also illegal for them to obtain medications over the Internet. Not to mention the fact that it is easier to avoid getting caught by avoiding the Internet! Common sense goes a long way in this discussion. A child that is smart enough to get their parent's credit card and decide to use it on the Internet has many choices in what to purchase. So you really think non-recreational prescription medications can compete with toys, games, videos, pornography, guns, and sex? Not a chance! Do you really think a kid wants to risk prosecution and imprisonment for prescription medication with no street value? If a kid uses a fake ID in order to buy alcohol, he can be fined and face jail time. It is much easier to catch a kid that uses a credit card, Fed Express, and fills out a computer consult. The only kids ordering prescription medications are going to be those kids asked to do so by those opposed to Internet medicine. Sting operations already occur where kids are used to order prescriptions by giving false information in order to show government agencies that Internet medicine sites are a danger to our children. Give me a break. What would stop a kid from stealing prescription medications like narcotics from their own parents rather than risking getting caught on the Internet? Narcotics do have street value and I can tell you that this really does occur all of the time! Emergency rooms see kids that have abused their parents prescription medications every week. Kids do have to be responsible for their actions by the way. If your child is caught shop lifting, they are prosecuted. The same punishment should be expected when they obtain prescriptions by giving false information. Internet medicine sites are very good about declaring that it is a Federal offense to give false information in order to obtain a prescription.

I hope my views have not given you a negative impression of me. Many people thought I should not discuss my views or skeletons because of the negative impact this could have on the readers. I disagreed with them and put the section in anyway. I will finish this book by updating you on all of the recent news stories, studies, and regulatory changes that have occurred since I started writing this book almost eight months ago.

SINCE WRITING THIS BOOK

A lot has happened since I started writing this book in February of 1999. I would like to briefly update you on some of the most pertinent news stories, medical studies, and regulatory changes that have occurred since this book started. Phen-Fen came up recently, when a Texas woman was awarded over 20 million dollars by a jury that wanted to punish American Home Products for allowing people to use Phen-Fen. Interestingly, her own cardiologist admitted that she had heart valve problems before taking Phen-Fen and that Phen-Fen probably did not have anything to do with her heart valve problems. Then a new study, which was published in the October of 1999 issue of the American Journal of Cardiology, declared that Fen-Phen patients did not develop heart valve disease from the medication. It was even admitted in the Journal that previous studies were in error and sloppily done! However, American Home Products still gave in to the pressures of all of the law suits it has been forced to defend and offered a settlement of over 3 billion dollars to put these suits behind it. Reminds me a lot of the breast implant fiasco that resulted in all of those class action suits against Dow... only later to find out that the implants caused no harm. What a country we live in! I said it earlier in this book and I will say it again: Fen-Phen was not dangerous and should not have been taken off of the market. Companies like American Home Products have had to pay a high price settlement because of this country's misunderstanding of the serious dangers associated with obesity. Obesity is far more dangerous and expensive than Fen-Phen. Remember that obesity kills 300,000 people annually in this country & Fen-Phen was probably saving tens of thousands of lives every year before these ridiculous accusations came out with regards to Fen-Phen causing heart valve abnormalities. Two other recent reports about obesity also support my contention that we need to take obesity much more seriously. The first was released by the American

Obesity Assoc. and this report indicated that healthcare costs to treat obese adults in this country exceeded $238 billion this year alone. The second came out of the New England Journal of Medicine and was conducted by the American Cancer Society. They concluded that obesity decreases your life span. This study is most gratifying to me because it justifies my contention that people need to be on medications before they have a BMI of 30. Many states including Ohio still maintain that people do not need medication until their BMI is 27 if they already have a co-morbid condition like hypertension or diabetes. It is also maintained that they don't need medication until they have a BMI of 30 if they have no co-morbid conditions. This new study shows that people with a BMI of 25 die sooner than those that are not overweight! It is even proclaimed that obesity is the second leading cause of preventable death…only exceeded by smoking. I find it very ironic that class action suits have been so successful against Dow and American Home Products and yet, no class action suits have been filed against the doctors and medical agencies that allow obesity to propagate. At least with obesity, unlike breast implants and Fen-Phen, we know that people really do have serious medical problems or die if not appropriately treated. The medical community has been confused about what needs to be eradicated and what needs to be accepted. Obesity needs to be eradicated and Internet medicine needs acceptance, not vice versa. We have made Tobacco companies responsible for the atrocities caused by cigarette smoking. Shouldn't we make physicians, Medical Boards, and Pharmacy Boards responsible for the atrocities caused by obesity? Physicians seem to be more interested in protecting their livelihood than they are in treating disease. Physicians are talking about starting their own union. I read recently that the AMA is now attacking herbals because they don't think they are safe! If they get their way, Americans will not be able to get herbals without a prescription! That sounds very good for doctors and very bad for Americans. I believe that many of the herbal remedies that have been around for hundreds of years really do work and that they have become a threat to physicians. Why? You don't need to spend money seeing a physician in order to get herbals. Pharmaceutical companies are also threatened because they lose revenue when people choose herbals rather than prescription medications! I have always said that if grass was found to have any pharmaceutical value to treat disease that pharmaceutical companies would somehow convince the government to ban citizens from growing grass in their yard. Imagine what would happen if our children started to eat grass, etc... That is exactly what is going to happen with herbal remedies that have been used safely for over one hundred years. Suddenly, they will be found to be dangerous and in need of regulation.

The final bit of news since I began writing this book pertains to some new regulations that have forced me to stop practicing Internet medicine as of October 1_{st} of 1999. The State Medical Board of Ohio has come up with some new regulations to get Internet medicine banned in Ohio and they became effective on October 1, 1999. I have printed them in their entirety in appendix D for your entertainment. They basically say that it is OK for all Ohio doctors to treat patients without seeing them or examining them, except for Internet medicine physicians like me. It is acceptable for a physician to prescribe medications to a patient without examining or seeing the patient if the physician is on call or cross covering for other physicians. It is also acceptable to prescribe medications if they are treating new patients they have not seen yet, or if the patient is in an institution such as a nursing home or hospital, or if some sort of protocol has already been established to treat patients. However, it is illegal for physicians like me to advertise my Internet business or prescribe to patients via the Internet. The fact that these regulations did not even exist until three months after my indictment suggests that I never did anything wrong by having an Internet medicine practice. I was indicted because I was prescribing medications to patients that I had not seen or examined in my Internet medicine practice. The State Medical Board of Ohio has now admitted that Ohio physicians often do the same thing that I do with my practice. I am not surprised that these people were able to make such regulations without getting any input from those physicians that practice Internet medicine or those patients that have utilized the Internet to get their treatment. The State Medical Board of Ohio has openly admitted that physicians often prescribe medications to patients that they do not examine or see. They have now officially admitted that this type of practice is acceptable. It is acceptable because everyone has been doing it for years! They have chosen to discriminate against physicians like me, that practice Internet medicine while openly admitting that every other physician in Ohio has their approval to prescribe medications without seeing or examining the patient. They have thus made it impossible for Ohio physicians to compete with physicians from other states for Ohio residents on the Internet. For instance, I will not be allowed to treat Ohio residents via the Internet unless these residents have been seen and examined by me personally. This does not prevent the Ohio resident from getting on the Internet and obtaining their medical treatment from physicians licensed in other states. Why would an Ohio resident that already knows what is wrong with them, come to my office for me to examine them so they can use my Internet site? I wouldn't! They will simply choose a different Internet site where the physician is not required to see and examine them prior to treating their medical illness. Remember that these people already know what is wrong with them! From a business perspective, there is no way I can compete with other Internet sites that don't require a personal visit to the physician prior to obtaining a prescription with an online medical consultation. The Ohio State Medical Board has basically discriminated against my business and me, so that I cannot practice Internet medicine. My civil rights have been violated. Your civil rights have also been violated. You should have the right to decide whether to see an Internet physician or go to a traditional doctor at his office. I should have the right to choose an Internet rather than a traditional practice. You cannot ban Internet medicine without some justification. The Ohio State Medical Board has used the same approach for regulating Internet medicine that it used for regulating the treatment of obesity. In both cases, they have been more concerned about themselves and their fellow physicians than they have been for the patients. When will Ohio residents stand up and do something about these atrocities? I would say that there is no better time than now. Ohio residents deserve to have some input into whether or not they want Internet medicine. I am certain that Ohio residents hate the weight-loss regulations after being informed about obesity and those regulations in this book. If someone acquires poison ivy while camping, it is OK for an Ohio physician to call in a prescription for that person without seeing or examining them as long as the physician schedules that patient for a future visit so that the patient can be examined and diagnosed. However, I am not allowed to treat that patient via the Internet because there is no future visit or examination! The treatment by the way consists of 7-14 days of steroids. If you had poison ivy, wouldn't you want the choice of ordering your medicine via the Internet or actually making an appointment and seeing the doctor? What if you are bald and want the latest prescription medication to treat it? Even worse, what if you have chronic herpes and don't want the medical staff to find out about it? Why should you be denied the opportunity to utilize an Ohio Internet physician when your family doctor is allowed to prescribe medications to people without ever seeing them? Talk about hypocrisy. On the positive side, these new regulations point out what I have been saying throughout this book. Physicians have been treating people with prescriptions for years without ever seeing or examining them! These new regulations seem to be saying that this practice can be condoned for traditional doctors with their traditional practices. However, it cannot be condoned in an Internet practice. Is this regulation being implemented to protect Ohio residents? Of course not! The new regulations are there to protect Ohio physicians, not Ohio residents. Fortunately for Ohio residents, they can still get Internet medical treatment from non-Ohio physicians. If Ohio residents don't complain, other states will soon follow suit with Ohio in implementing regulations that stop physicians from their respective states from practicing Internet Medicine. Eventually, every state will prohibit its own physicians from this type of practice. Then people will not have the Internet option available to them. We need to get these regulations changed now, before every state follows Ohio's lead.

Ohio residents with obesity that have been inappropriately treated deserve more than simple regulatory changes. They deserve financial retribution for their suffering, medical bills, and pain. Instead of suing the drug companies that have developed appropriate medications to treat obesity, people need to sue those responsible for the discrimination and inappropriate treatment of obesity. Obviously, that would be those agencies and physicians that have failed to take obesity seriously. In Ohio, it is safe to say that the State Pharmacy and Medical Boards would be at the top of that list, followed by those personal physicians that have not taken obesity seriously.

This pretty much concludes this book and I sincerely hope that my words have persuaded many of you to side with me on the issues of obesity and Internet medicine. I will be in court within the next several months defending my views against Ohio's State Pharmacy Board. The State Medical board will also be actively attempting to take away my medical license because of my past practice of Internet medicine. You can defend my views with your own families, friends, co-workers, etc…Unlike me, you are not risking imprisonment for defending these issues. I am going to give you my post office box address so that I can receive your feedback on this book. I expect that many of you will have something to say about at least one of the topics that I have addressed and I look forward to hearing from you! You can also check out my web sites at www.rxclinic.com and www.Eprescribe.com to obtain your own opinion on the safety of my Internet sites. Although I am no longer the physician that prescribes on these sites, I can assure you that the active physician is a licensed and conscientious individual that also believes that Internet medicine is safe, private, and convenient.

My address is:
Daniel Thompson, M.D.
4856 Sawmill Rd. PMB# 307
Columbus, Ohio 43235

Epilogue

I have been indicted for selling and trafficking dangerous drugs, based on evidence gathered by the Ohio State Pharmacy Board. I will be tried and possibly jailed for the way I practice medicine. Ohio does not feel that my online consultation has been adequate enough for me to consider my Internet patients to be "real" patients. In fact, they don't even consider me to be a real physician when I do Internet medicine. Thus, they are currently calling my patients at their homes and offices to ask them detailed questions about their diseases and their interactions with me. We were horrified to find this out because many of these clients have sexual dysfunction or herpes and their lives would be ruined if this private information became public.

We had our attorney make a request to the prosecuting attorney for an immediate stop to the calling and harassing of these patients because of the danger of others finding out about their personal and private medical history. I really did take the Hippocratic oath and I do believe that a patient's medical history is private and confidential. At the time of this writing, my patients continue to be called by these people.

This act alone proves to me that these agencies have no interest in the welfare of my Internet patients. At least $50,000 in our business account has been frozen by these agencies and we voluntarily stopped the operation of those Internet sites involved in this case. I have written the ACLU asking for help in protecting my patients' medical history from being leaked by these Ohio agencies. I have currently paid $100,000 for legal fees to defend Internet medicine and, of course, myself.

My career has been virtually destroyed, my business devastated, and my honesty questioned, but you see I am not afraid to fight. I only want that fight to be a fair fight! This book is one of the weapons that will allow me to even the odds so that it is a fair fight. I will continue to bluntly bash those parts of the medical field that deserve it, to promote the treatment of obesity, and to bring Internet medicine into the twenty-first century.

Appendix A

Ohio Weight Loss Rules

The State Medical Board of Ohio adopted the following rules at its October 14, 1998 Board meeting: Rules 4731-11-01, 4731-11-03, 4731-11-04, effective October 31, 1998; and Rules 4731-11-08 and 4731-21-01 through 4731-21-06, effective November 11, 1998. The rules are printed here in their entirety.

4731-11-01, 4731-11-03, 4731-11-04, 4731-11-08, 4731-21-01, 4731-21-02, 4731-21-03, 4731-21-04, 4731-21-05, 4731-21-06

4731-11-01 Definitions.

As used in Chapter 4731-11 of the Administrative Code:

(A) "Controlled substance" means a drug, compound, mixture, preparation, or substance included in schedule I, II, III, IV, or V pursuant to the provisions of Chapter 3719. of the Revised Code.

(B) "Controlled substance stimulant" means any drug, compound, mixture, preparation, or substance which is classified as a stimulant in controlled substance schedule II, III, or IV listed in section 3719.41 of the Revised Code, or which is classified as a stimulant in controlled substances schedule II, III, or IV pursuant to section 3719.43 or 3719.44 of the Revised Code.

(C) "Utilize a controlled substance or controlled substance stimulant" means to prescribe, administer, dispense, supply, sell or give a controlled substance or controlled substance stimulant.

(D) "Recognized contraindication" means any contraindication to the use of a drug which is listed in the United States food and drug administration (hereinafter, "F.D.A.") approved labeling for the drug, or which the board determines to be accepted as a contraindication.

(E) "The board" means the state medical board of Ohio.

(F) "BMI" means body mass index, calculated as a person's weight in kilograms divided by height in meters squared.

Eff. 10/31/98

4731-11-03 Schedule II controlled substance stimulants.

(A) A physician shall not utilize a schedule II controlled substance stimulant for any purpose except:

(1) The treatment of narcolepsy;

(2) The treatment or abnormal behavioral syndrome (attention deficit disorder, hyperkinetic syndrome), and/or related disorders of childhood;

(3) The treatment of drug-induced or trauma-induced brain dysfunction;

(4) The differential diagnostic psychiatric evaluation of depression;

(5) The treatment of depression shown to be refractory to other therapeutic modalities, including pharmacologic approaches, such as tricyclic antidepressants and MAO inhibitors;

(6) As adjunctive therapy in the treatment of chronic severe pain or depression, in the terminal stages of diseases which are accompanied by severe pain;

(7) The clinical investigation of the effects of such drugs, in which case the physician shall submit to the board a written investigative protocol for its review and approval before the investigation has begun. The investigation shall be conducted in strict compliance with the investigative protocol, and the physician shall, within sixty days following the conclusion of the investigation, submit to the board a written report detailing the findings and conclusions of the investigation.

(B) A physician shall not utilize a schedule II controlled substance stimulant for purposes of weight reduction or control.

(C) A physician may utilize a schedule II controlled substance stimulant when properly indicated for any purpose listed in paragraph (A) of this rule, provided that all of the following conditions are met:

(1) Before initiating treatment utilizing a schedule II controlled substance stimulant, the physician obtains a thorough history, performs a thorough physical examination of the patient, and rules out the existence of any recognized contraindications to the use of the controlled substance stimulant to be utilized.

(2) The physician shall not utilize any schedule II controlled substance stimulant when he knows or has reason to believe that a recognized contra-indication to its use exists.

(3) The physician shall not utilize any schedule II controlled substance stimulant in the treatment of a patient who he knows or should know is pregnant.

(4) Upon ascertaining or having reason to believe that the patient has a history of or shows a propensity for alcohol or drug abuse, or that the patient has consumed or disposed of any controlled substance other than in strict compliance with the treating physician's directions, the physician shall reappraise the desirability of continued utilization of schedule II controlled substance stimulants and shall document in the patient record the factors weighed in deciding to continue their use. The physician shall actively monitor such a patient for signs and symptoms of drug abuse and drug dependency.

(D) A violation of any provision of this rule, as determined by the board, shall constitute "failure to use reasonable care discrimination in the administration of drugs," as that clause is used in division (B)(2) of section 4731.22 of the Revised Code; "selling, prescribing, giving away, or administering drugs for other than legal and legitimate therapeutic purposes," as that clause is used in division (B)(3) of section 4731.22 of the Revised Code; and "a departure from, or the failure to conform to, minimal standards of care of similar practitioners under the same or similar circumstances, whether or not actual injury to a patient is established," as that clause is used in division (B)(6) of section 4731.22 of the Revised Code.

Eff. 10/31/98

4731-11-04 Controlled substances: utilization for weight reduction.

(A) A physician shall not utilize a schedule III or IV controlled substance for purposes of weight reduction unless it has an F.D.A. approved indication for this purpose and then only in accordance with all of the provisions of this rule.

(B) The appropriate utilization of controlled substances to assist in weight reduction requires continuing interaction between the physician and the patient to assess the patient's dedication to the treatment program, response to treatment, freedom from signs of drug or alcohol abuse, and the presence or absence of contraindications and adverse side effects. The physician shall personally meet face-to-face with the patient each time controlled substances are utilized for weight reduction, and shall record in the patient record information demonstrating the patient's continuing efforts to lose weight and the presence or absence of contraindications, adverse effects, and indicators of possible substance abuse that would necessitate cessation of treatment utilizing controlled substances.

(C) A physician may utilize a schedule III or IV controlled substance for purposes of weight reduction in the treatment of obesity only as an adjunct, in accordance with the F.D.A. approved labeling for the product, in a regimen of weight reduction based on caloric restriction, provided that all of the following conditions are met:

(1) Before initiating treatment utilizing a schedule III or IV controlled substance, the physician determines through review of the physician's own records of prior treatment, or through review of the records of prior treatment which another treating physician or weight-loss program has provided to the physician, that the patient has made a substantial good-faith effort to lose weight in a treatment program utilizing a regimen of weight reduction based on caloric restriction, nutritional counseling, behavior modification, and exercise, without the utilization of controlled substances, and that said treatment has been ineffective.

(2) Before initiating treatment utilizing a schedule III or IV controlled substance, the physician obtains a thorough history, performs a thorough physical examination

of the patient, determines that the patient has a BMI of at least thirty, or at least twenty-seven with comorbid factors, and rules out the existence of any recognized contraindications to the use of the controlled substance to be utilized.

(3) The physician shall not utilize any schedule III or IV controlled substance when the physician knows or has reason to believe that a recognized contraindication to its use exists.

(4) The physician shall not utilize any schedule III or IV controlled substance for purposes of weight reduction in the treatment of a patient the physician knows or should know is pregnant.

(5) Except as provided in paragraph (D) of this rule, the physician shall not initiate or shall discontinue utilizing all schedule III or IV controlled substances that do not bear F.D.A. approved labeling which permits long-term use immediately upon ascertaining or having reason to believe:

> (a) That the patient has failed to lose weight while under treatment with a controlled substance or controlled substances over a period of thirty days during the current course of treatment, which determination shall be made by weighing the patient at least every thirtieth day, except that a patient who has never before received treatment for obesity utilizing any controlled substance who fails to lose weight during the

first thirty days of his first such treatment attempt may be treated for an additional thirty days; or

(b) That the patient has repeatedly failed to comply with the physician's treatment recommendations.

(6) The physician shall not initiate or shall discontinue utilizing all controlled substances for purposes of weight reduction immediately upon ascertaining or having reason to believe:

(a) That the patient has a history of or shows a propensity for alcohol or drug abuse, or has made any false or misleading statement to the physician relating to the patient's use of drugs or alcohol; or

(b) That the patient has consumed or disposed of any controlled substance other than in strict compliance with the treating physician's directions.

(7) Except as provided in paragraph (D) of this rule, the physician shall not resume utilizing a controlled substance following an interruption of treatment of more than seven days unless the f.d.a. approved labeling for the product permits long-term use, or unless the interruption resulted from one or more of the following:

(a) Illness of or injury to the patient justifying a temporary cessation of treatment; or

(b) Unavailability of the physician; or

(c) Unavailability of the patient, if the patient has notified the physician of the cause of the patient's unavailability.

(8) If the FDA approved labeling of the controlled substance being utilized for weight loss states that it is indicated for use for "a few weeks", the total course of treatment using that controlled substance shall not exceed twelve weeks.

(9) After initiating treatment, the physician may elect to switch to a different controlled substance for weight loss based on sound medical judgment, but the total course of treatment for any combination of controlled substances each of which is indicated for "a few weeks" shall not exceed twelve weeks.

(10) The physician may continue to utilize a schedule III or IV controlled substance in the treatment of a patient who has ceased to lose weight during a course of treatment only if all of the following conditions are met:

(a) The patient was morbidly obese, having a bmi of at least thirty-five, at the start of treatment;

(b) The patient exhibited a comorbid factor, such as uncontrolled diabetes, that did not respond to standard treatment measures but improved or is reasonably expected to improve while under treatment with controlled substances to an extent that significantly reduces risk of mortality;

(c) Continued treatment will not violate paragraph (C)(6) of this rule;

(d) The F.D.A. approved labeling for the controlled substance being utilized permits maintenance use;

(e) The patient lost at least five percent of initial body weight before weight loss stopped and has maintained that weight loss, which determination shall be made by weighing the patient at least every thirtieth day. If a patient receiving maintenance treatment under this paragraph has maintained weight loss of less than five percent of initial body weight at a required weighing, the physician shall cease utilizing controlled substances to assist the patient's weight loss, and may initiate a new course of treatment utilizing controlled substances only in accordance with paragraph (D) of this rule. If the physician stops maintenance treatment utilizing controlled substances in order to determine whether the patient can maintain weight loss unassisted by controlled substances, the patient's failure to maintain weight loss of at least five percent of initial body weight shall not prohibit reinstitution of treatment using controlled substances.

(D) Unless prohibited by paragraph (C)(6) of this rule, a physician may initiate a new course of treatment utilizing a controlled substance for purposes of weight reduction if the patient has not received any controlled substance for purposes of weight reduction within the past six months.

(E) A violation of any provision of this rule, as determined by the board, shall constitute "failure to use reasonable care discrimination in the administration of drugs," as that clause is used in DIVISION (B)(2) of section 4731.22 of the Revised Code; "selling, prescribing, giving away, or administering drugs for other than legal and legitimate therapeutic purposes," as that clause is used in division (B)(3) of section 4731.22 of the Revised Code; and "a departure from, or the failure to conform to, minimal standards of care of similar practitioners under the same or similar circumstances, whether or not actual injury to a patient is established," as that clause is used in division (B)(6) of section 4731.22 of the Revised Code.

Eff. 10/31/98

Appendix B

CYBER DOC
Internet Medicine, Physicians and You

By Daniel Thompson, M.D.
March 1999

TABLE OF CONTENTS

Introduction 154
Internet medicine 155
It Isn't for Everyone 158
But It Is for Some People 159
The Medical Process 160
Self-Evident Conditions 161
A Few Words about Obesity 162
Getting Medications over the Internet 164
Regulating Internet medicine 166
Some Last Thoughts 168

Introduction

The Internet is influencing nearly every aspect of our lives. It has already had a profound impact on the way we work, gather information and communicate with each other. Currently, it's reshaping another aspect of our society: how we do business with one another.

"E-commerce," as it's often called, was relatively uncommon just a few years ago. Now, however, the idea is picking up steam, and the practice of buying all kinds of products over the Internet is accelerating at an incredible rate. For instance, in an online article, Commerce Secretary William Daley said that sales on the Internet were around $9 billion for 1998.1 The types of products that can be bought over the Internet are increasing, as well. These days, you can buy all kinds of products through the Internet, from books to clothing, and from sofas to prescription medications.

That last item, purchasing prescription medications over the Internet, is what this booklet is about.

My name is Daniel Thompson, and I've been a physician for 15 years, since 1983. I am board certified in Internal Medicine. I practiced emergency medicine for 13 years and currently am involved in bariatric medicine (weight loss). For the last two years, I've owned and operated several weight loss centers in Columbus, Ohio. In addition, since September of 1998, I have been practicing Internet medicine. I currently have two Web sites where already-diagnosed patients can get FDA-approved prescription medications for certain conditions.

I've written this booklet because I believe that patients have the right to know about what is available to them through the Internet. This booklet expresses my personal experiences and beliefs; I don't claim that it represents the opinions of the medical community in general.

Internet Medicine

As I mentioned a moment ago, the Internet is influencing many aspects of our lives (and it's beginning to affect how patients have access to medications. The Internet is already having a revolutionary effect on medicine as we know it, even changing how patients interact with their doctors. But that's a whole other topic! For this discussion, let's stick to the Internet and prescription medications.

The combination of medicine and the Internet is fairly recent and, like a lot of new ideas, it's somewhat controversial. Many physicians and professional medical organizations are concerned about the potential abuse of access to drugs over the Internet and about patients being treated without seeing a doctor. These are understandable concerns, but I believe they are misplaced and that there are important reasons why patients should be able to get certain medications via the Internet.

First of all, the abuse of prescription drugs doesn't require the Internet to happen (it happens all the time, anyway. It's very easy for a patient to continue getting prescriptions for a drug long after he or she has stopped physically needing it. For example, a patient who has a history of migraine headaches may continue to see their physician and request prescriptions for pain medication. The physician probably will continue to prescribe medication, despite the fact that there is no specific test she or he can give to determine whether the patient is still actually having migraines or just seeking pain medication. The physician must take the patient's word for it. I'm not saying that this abuse is OK (it isn't (but I am saying that, realistically, prescription abuse already exists, the Internet is not the cause of this problem. There will always be people who abuse prescription drugs (and doctors who allow them to), and they will find a way to do that, with or without the Internet.

As for giving prescription medication to someone without actually examining them, let me be very clear about this: In my Internet practice, I do not make diagnoses (the patients I treat over the Internet have already been diagnosed.

Let me add that prescribing prescription medication for patients without examining them is often done by physicians for certain conditions or under specific circumstances. For instance, physicians who don't actually see, examine or even talk to the patient receiving the medicine often prescribe prescription medications for chronic illness. Diabetics, asthmatics, chronic back injury victims and heart patients, for example, get prescription medications from physicians when their personal physicians are not available to refill their prescriptions. Physicians are often asked to call in a prescription for patients who run out of medication and aren't able to see their own physician right away. Most people either have had, or know someone who has had, a doctor call in a prescription without seeing them first.

I'm not saying this is necessarily a bad practice. The mother of a child who has chronic ear infections may not be able to get her child to the doctor every time a flare-up occurs. Or consider an asthmatic who is out of his inhaler, the soon-to-be bride who wants an antibiotic to prevent a bladder infection from ruining her honeymoon or someone who is going on a cruise and needs a scopolamine patch to prevent seasickness. In this day and age, it's extremely difficult for a physician to see every patient every time they need a prescription, yet it could be considered less than humanitarian to deny help to those who ask for it.

By filling such a request, the physician is not making a diagnosis per se ó the diagnosis has already been made in some of the above examples, such as the chronic ear infection and asthma. In the other examples, i.e., the potential bladder infection and the seasickness, there is no diagnosis to make because there is no disease present. In these examples, prevention is key. The bottom line here is that physicians are often willing to treat known diseases and/or prevent disease with prescription medication without actually seeing the patient. The physician does this because it is not always convenient or practical for these people to get to the physician's office and/or for the physician to get to his office at the time these people need their medicines.

The telephone, particularly the cell phone, has made this practice even easier by allowing physicians to have more time out of the office. Physicians can now call in prescriptions from sporting events, golf courses, restaurants, church, etc.

As convenient as this type of medical practice can be, however, is does create some problems. Physicians can't be reimbursed for it, and they have no permanent, hard-copy record of who has been treated and what medication they were treated with. They also have limited access to a patient's history, including allergies, current medications and prior illnesses.

Internet medicine allows physicians and patients the convenience of treating simple, common, recurring ailments without either party having to be at the physician's office, yet it also provides doctors with records of who they treat and how, as well as with patients' medical histories.

What many people, including many doctors, don't understand about Internet medicine (the prescription of medications over the Internet (is that this service is at the end of a long medical process.

It Isn't for Everyone

I'll talk more about that process in awhile, but first I need to point out that Internet medicine is not for everyone. There are two very important reasons for this. One is about medicine and the other is about the Internet.

The first reason is that when we are injured or feeling bad, we need doctors to figure out how serious the injury is or what is making us sick, and also how to make us feel better (in other words, to make a diagnosis and determine a treatment. No ethical physician will give a diagnosis or determine treatment over the Internet because giving people prescription medications without first having a diagnosis can be very dangerous.

The second reason is a little more complicated, and it has to do with the very nature of the Internet. The Internet and World Wide Web are the potentially most grassroots democratic forces in the world (anyone who has access to a computer can get on them and get information or give out information. You can be anyone you say you are, and you can say or do just about anything you want — in other words, the Internet provides a tremendous amount of individual freedom and power.

The advantages of this are obvious, but there's a down side, too: All of that individual freedom demands an equal amount of individual responsibility. For instance, you probably already know that you can't assume that everything you see or read on every Web page is true. As I mentioned before, anyone can say anything on the Internet — literally — so it's up to you to figure out which sources of information are reputable and accurate, and which aren't.

With Internet medicine, you have to be responsible for yourself in two ways. You have to figure out which medications Web sites are safe, but you also have to be responsible about how you use the services they offer. What do I mean by that? I mean that it's up to you to see a physician and get a diagnosis and treatment plan before you log on and order medication. As I said before, the diagnosis of an injury or illness cannot yet be made over the Internet.

BUT IT IS FOR SOME PEOPLE

OK, we've talked about who Internet medicine isn't for, but who is it for? There are several groups of people who can safely use the Internet to get prescription medications. First, there are people who've been through the diagnosis and treatment determination process and already have a known diagnosis (such as diabetes, hypertension, asthma, arthritis, obesity, etc.). Second, there are people who have self-evident, or obvious, conditions (such as being addicted to nicotine, going bald, or having acne or increased wrinkles due to aging) or who need medication for preventive reasons (such as the Epi pen for people with known severe allergies to things like peanuts and bee stings, or scopolamine patches for the prevention of motion sickness).

Finally, there are people who suffer from sexual dysfunction and recurrent genital herpes — embarrassing diseases that effect millions of men and women.

THE MEDICAL PROCESS

Let's talk about the first group of people, which means discussing the medical process I mentioned earlier. As I've already said, getting prescription medications over the Internet comes at the end of the diagnosis and treatment determination process that patients must go through. That process begins with seeing a physician to figure out why you don't feel well. It continues when the physician uses a systematic approach to find out what's wrong with you. Any good physician will get your medical history and give you a physical exam, which probably will include having tests done (such as blood tests, EKGs and X rays), then make a diagnosis and determine the most effective treatment. Let's look at this process in a little more detail:

1. *The Medical History.* This is the information about what health problems our relatives may have, what health problems we may already have, what allergies we may have and what medications we may be on.

2. *The Physical Examination.* This includes taking your vital signs (blood pressure, pulse or heart rate, and breathing rate); looking in your ears, nose and throat; listening to your heart, lungs and abdomen; feeling your throat, neck, underarms, abdomen and chest; and doing a digital rectal examination and (for women) a pelvic examination. The physical exam can help a physician determine what is wrong with a patient. For instance, listening to the heart or lungs may help a physician diagnose heart disease or pneumonia.

Looking at a patient's ears and throat can help a doctor figure out whether an infection is present.

3. *Tests.* Your physician may have various tests done to get more information about what's wrong with you. Common tests are blood tests, EKGs (electrocardiograms, which give information about the heart) and X-rays. Many infections, cancers and other diseases cannot be determined without these and other tests.

4. *Making a Diagnosis.* Your physician uses the information obtained from all of the above steps to make a diagnosis — to figure out what's wrong with you.

5. *Determining a Treatment.* Once your doctor knows what the problem is, he or she determines the most effective treatment to help heal you. Usually, this means prescribing one or more medications to treat the disorder. Your physician decides which specific medications are best to treat your particular disease depending on what medications you're already on (if any) and what medications you're allergic to (if any). In other words, once a diagnosis has been made, the treatment is based on the patient's medical history. A physician uses steps 1-3 to make a diagnosis, then often uses step 1, the medical history, to determine treatment.

SELF-EVIDENT CONDITIONS

Now let's talk now about the second group of people, the people whose conditions are self-evident (obvious) or who require treatment to prevent morbidity (illness). For instance, a man who's suffering from male pattern baldness doesn't need to see a physician to figure out that he's losing his hair. Similarly, someone who has acne doesn't necessarily need to have it diagnosed by a dermatologist. And patients who know that they get motion sickness don't need an examination before being given a scopolamine patch before taking a long car trip or going on a cruise.

However, even people with obvious conditions should fill out a medical history before being prescribed medications over the Internet, and any reputable Internet medicine site should require a medical history and information about the medications being prescribed. No reputable physician should prescribe medications for you without knowing your medical history.

Finally, let's discuss treatment for people who suffer from sexual dysfunction and recurrent genital herpes, emotionally sensitive conditions that can be easily treated with prescription medication obtained over the Internet. I'm discussing them separately partly because they are not quite in the same league as baldness and acne, for instance. First, sexual dysfunction and herpes are very private, potentially embarrassing disorders. Second, sexual dysfunction may be not only a problem by itself, but also a symptom of other disease. Because it's so personal, many people who suffer from sexual dysfunction are much more comfortable getting medications over the Internet rather than seeing a physician. But because its causes might be complex and serious, you might want to see a doctor before getting medication for it over the Internet. Even if you decide not to see a physician first, you should certainly see one if the condition doesn't improve with treatment.

A Few Words about Obesity

Let's talk for a moment about people who suffer from obesity. obesity, like baldness, acne, smoking and sexual dysfunction, can be treated with prescription medications that can be obtained over the Internet. However, unlike those other conditions, obesity is potentially far more serious in terms of your general health. If you suffer from the disease of obesity — and it is a disease — you should see a physician at least once to have your condition and the proper course of treatment determined before you go to the Internet for prescription medication. You may have other medical problems, caused by the obesity, which could make it very dangerous for you to take certain medications.

There are many myths and prejudices surrounding the disease of obesity. (For medical purposes, 'obesity" is defined as being 30 percent or more over one's ideal weight.) The most common myth is that people are obese because they are lazy and eat too much. Yet, most of us know at least one person who can eat everything in sight, never exercise and yet not gain weight. On the other hand, there are athletes who are absolutely obese, by medical standards, yet who exercise more than 90 percent of Americans and who are superbly physically fit. One of the facts that has been discovered through scientific research is that obesity — or the lack of it — is often genetic. In other words, obesity may have as much, or more, to do with your family genes than with what you eat and how much you exercise.

But whatever the causes of obesity, the fact remains that it is a potentially deadly disease. A normal-weight individual is 280 times less likely to die than an individual who is 100 pounds over their ideal weight. obesity increases the risk of asthma, coronary artery disease, adult onset diabetes, hypertension, cancer, gall bladder disease, etc. It causes morbidity (disease) and mortality (death), and it needs to be taken seriously and treated systematically, like any other disease.

Unfortunately, ignorant prejudices about obesity are as common in the medical community as they are in the general population. Those of you who are afflicted with obesity probably have encountered at least one doctor, if not several, who believes that being overweight is your fault and your problem, and that all you need to do is eat less and exercise more to lose weight. This is often not the case, however. Don't misunderstand me — eating healthily and getting exercise is important for everyone. But for individuals who suffer from obesity, proper medication can make all the difference in determining whether or not a patient can successfully lose weight.

Because physicians and medical organizations are often prejudiced about obesity and about effective treatments for it, they can make it difficult for patients to get medications for their condition. For example, I live in Ohio, where the state medical board recently made it tougher to treat obesity than in almost any other state in the U.S. Ohio physicians are now required to stop the treatment (medication) after the disease is under control. Yet, once the excess weight has been lost, medication is required to maintain the new, normal weight. Can you imagine having to stop your insulin after your blood sugar returns to normal, or discontinuing your blood pressure medication after your blood pressure returns to normal levels?

Getting Medications over the Internet

Assuming that a qualified physician has already diagnosed you as having a particular condition and has determined

APPENDIX

proper treatment for that condition, or that you have an easily recognized condition, let's talk about the actual process of being on the Web and ordering the medications you need.

I operate legitimate Web sites (www.cybrx.com and www.get-it-on.com) where you will get an online medical consultation and can be prescribed FDA-approved medications for known and easily recognized disorders. (The medications can be shipped to your home or office for next-day delivery.) I treat patients online who have one of the following conditions:

Obesity
Male Pattern Baldness
Smoking Addiction
Recurrent Herpes
Sexual Dysfunction
Acne
Wrinkles

When you log on to one of these sites, you will be directed through the process of ordering your medication online. You will need to give your medical history online, and you'll be able to learn about the medications and to print out a form that you can complete before mailing or faxing it in.

I prescribe the following medications to treat their respective conditions: Viagra™ for sexual dysfunction, Valtrex for recurrent herpes, Propecia™ for male hair loss (women who are, or may be, pregnant must not use or even touch this medication, because it causes deformity in unborn male babies), Meridia™ and Phentermine for obesity, and Zyban™ for smoking. We will soon be using

Renova to treat wrinkles and Retin A to treat acne.

A question patients often have about ordering medications over the Internet is whether or not it's safe to use a credit card for online purchases. Yes, it's safe. This is because many online companies, including mine, uses what are called 'secure servers," which encrypt, or disguise, your credit card information so that it can't be recognized by anyone but the recipient. (Frankly, you're at greater risk using your card at a restaurant, for instance, where any employee can write down your card information while the card is out of your site.) Also, all cards have a limit on the amount of fraudulent use for which you're liable, and the most they can hold you responsible for, if you're a U.S. resident, is $50.2 (One warning, however: A debit card, or check card, is not a credit card, even if it carries a MasterCard or VISA logo. Debit cards are not protected with the same legislation, and I caution you not to use your debit card on the Internet.3)

Regulating Internet Medicine

Because Internet medicine is new and controversial, some physicians and professional medical organizations would prefer to ban it completely. It is already too late to do that, however. This is partly because of the nature of the Internet itself and partly because the Internet is already being used for various medical functions.

The nature of the Internet means that it has no borders (if the medical boards in half of the states in the U.S. ban physicians from practicing Internet medicine, but the other states don't, patients will just do business on Web sites based in states where Internet medicine is legal. This would be true even if 49 out of 50 states criminalized Internet medicine. Even if every state banned the practice of Internet medicine, that couldn't stop patients from getting medications over the Internet from other countries (which already happens, by the way).

In addition, the Internet is already being used for a variety of medical, and even surgical, functions. Telemedicine is an excellent example. Essentially, telemedicine is the electronic transfer of patient information through telecommunications and information technologies for the purpose of improving access to, and quality of, health care in underserved areas. Telemedicine has been used since the 1960s, but with the advent of the Internet, these days telemedicine usually offers video consulting by computer. For instance, telemedicine enables surgeons who are hundreds of miles away from the site of an operation to supervise the procedure via the Internet. The government has funded telemedicine programs in many states, including Ohio. In addition, radiology (X-rays) is already being practiced by computer in almost every state.

While telemedicine and electronic radiology don't include the sale of prescription medications over the Internet, virtual pharmacies, such as Drugstore.com and PlanetRx, have recently come online (or are about to come online, as of this writing). These companies sell a variety of health and beauty products over the Internet, including prescription medications. All of these examples point to the same conclusion: Internet medicine is here to stay.

Because we cannot get rid of Internet medicine, we should regulate it. This is necessary to make sure that physicians with bad records or who make false claims about the medications they sell cannot practice on the Internet. Narcotics should not be dispensed unless they are an approved treatment for a particular disease. Currently, these kinds of consumer protections don't exist in Internet medicine.

SOME LAST THOUGHTS

I firmly believe that Cyber Doc is going to be a part of the 21st century for the same reasons that people talk with each other, work and shop online: It's convenient and private. Obviously, the Internet does not and cannot replace physicians and emergency rooms in acute cases such as heart attacks, broken bones, gunshot wounds, etc. Nor can current Internet medical sites diagnose disease. But for patients who are not acutely injured or ill and who understand what they need to treat ailments they already know they have — especially if those diagnoses include sexual dysfunction, obesity, hair loss, nicotine addiction or recurrent genital herpes — Internet medicine is a wonderfully convenient, private way to obtain needed medications.

1 Kane, Margaret. 'Feds will track Web sales," ZDNet, Feb. 5, 1999
2 Levine, John R. and Carol Baroudi and Margaret Levine Young. The Internet for Dummies. (Foster City, Calif.: IDG Books Worldwide, 1998)
3 Ibid

APPENDIX C

References

#1. Obesity kills several hundred thousand Americans annually: (JAMA, 1996;276:1907-1915) Up to 300,000 people die every year in this country because of obesity. This same statistic has also been quoted by the former US Surgeon General, Dr. C. Everett Koop. This same statistic is quoted in the document titled Physical Activity and Good Nutrition: 1999; which is published by the Centers for Disease Control and Prevention (CDC).

#2. Obesity increases your risk of getting heart disease: The American Heart Association now considers obesity a major risk factor for the development of coronary artery disease. It is one of the association's major risk factors that people can control to prevent coronary disease and the associated heart attacks from coronary disease. It is ranked right up there with smoking, high cholesterol, and high blood pressure.

#3. Over 50% of all Americans are now overweight: Taken from the National Health and Nutritional Examination Survey (NHANES) III, 1988-1994

#4. Obesity increases the risk of acquiring diabetes, asthma, cancer, gallbladder disease, high blood pressure, and coronary disease. Too many sources to mention! Will not be disputed by the AMA, AHA, or any government agency.

#5. 20% of children in this country are overweight. The number of obese children has doubled in the last 30 years and is now 20% according to the NHANES III.

#6. Obesity is a life-long disease. This is the stand of the American Heart Association and has been quoted by the vice chairman of the AHA's Nutritional Committee. It is also the stand of the American Society of Bariatric physicians. These and many more statistics can be verified by the American Society of Bariatric Physicians by calling: Tel: 303-770-2526 or Fax: 303-779-4834 or E-mail: bariatric@asbp.org and asking for information.

#7. Ohio has three of the top ten cities, when it comes to the prevalence of obesity in the USA. According to the 1997 National Weight Report, Cleveland, Columbus, and Cincinnati are ranked 5th, 7th, and 8th while New Orleans is #1.

#8. Indiana is #1 when it comes to the prevalence of obesity and Ohio is #8. According to the CDC (Centers for Disease Control and Prevention) Indiana is the heaviest state and Hawaii the leanest. Ohio ranks as the 8th heaviest behind Indiana, Alaska, Missouri, Michigan, West Virginia, Mississippi, and Iowa—listed in order from heaviest to lightest. The alarming thing about this survey is that Ohio only has 0.5% less people overweight than the #2 ranked heaviest state of Alaska. In fact, a second survey published recently by the CDC ranks Ohio #5! Also of interest in this second survey is that Indiana is no longer even in the top 10— it is 12th! Why? I believe it is because they got rid of their strict weight loss rules!

#9. Diabetes and obesity are often related. Many studies reveal that 90% of all diabetics have adult onset diabetes. Also 8 or 9 out of every 10 adult onset diabetics are obese! 90% of all adult onset diabetics are overweight. The American Diabetes Association will stand by those statistics. Does Ohio have many diabetics? It ranks 2nd in the nation for having the highest death rates for diabetes and 7th in the number of adults with diagnosed diabetes.

#10. Weight loss medications have no street value and are not addictive. The American Society of Bariatric Physicians (ASBP) had an investigator contact Drug Enforcement Agency (DEA) offices in the major US cities to see if they had any problem with Phentermine (Adipex) or Meridia™. There were no cities that had reported any arrests or problems relating to these medications. In fact, they claimed that these drugs did not seem to have any street value! This is interesting, since anyone in this country can get narcotics from a physician to treat back pain, migraine headaches, arthritis, etc— and these medications have marked street value.

#11. Fen-Phen didn't cause heart valve damage after all! According to a new study published in the Journal of the American College of Cardiology, there is no evidence that Fen-Phen caused heart valve abnormalities.

#12. Obesity decreases your life span. The October of 99' issue of the New England Journal of Medicine contains a study done by the American Cancer Society that shows a decrease in life span for those people that are overweight. Even those with a BMI as low as 25 tend to have a decreased life span!

Appendix D

New Ohio regulations related to the Internet

4731-11-09 Prescribing to persons not seen by the physician.
(A) Except in institutional settings, on call situations, cross coverage situations, situations involving new patients, protocol situations, and situations involving nurses practicing in accordance with standard care arrangements, as described in paragraphs (D) and (E) of this rule, a physician shall not prescribe, dispense, or otherwise provide, or cause to be provided, any controlled substance to a person who the physician has never personally physically examined and diagnosed.

(B) Except in institutional settings, on call situations, cross coverage situations, situations involving new patients, protocol situations, and situations involving nurses practicing in accordance with standard care arrangements, as described in paragraphs (D) and (E) of this rule, a physician shall not prescribe, dispense, or otherwise provide, or cause to be provided, any dangerous drug which is not a controlled substance to a person who the physician has never personally physically examined and diagnosed, except in accordance with the following requirements:

(1) The physician is providing care in consultation with another physician who has an ongoing professional relationship with the patient, and who has agreed to supervise the patient's use of the drug or drugs to be provided; and

(2) The physician's care of the patient meets all applicable standards of care and all applicable statutory and regulatory requirements.

(C) A physician shall not advertise or offer, or permit the physician's name or certificate to be used in an advertisement or offer, to provide any dangerous drug in a manner that would violate paragraph (A) or paragraph (B) of this rule.

(D) Paragraphs (A) and (B) of this rule do not apply to or prohibit the provision of drugs to a person who is admitted as an inpatient to or is a resident of an institutional facility. for purposes of this rule, "institutional facility" has the same meaning as in rule 4729-17-01 of the Administrative Code. This paragraph does not authorize or legitimize practices that would violate other applicable standards or legal requirements.

(E) Paragraphs (A) and (B) of this rule do not apply to or prohibit:

(1) The provision of controlled substances or dangerous drugs by a physician to a person who is a patient of a colleague of the physician, if the drugs are provided pursuant to an on call or cross coverage arrangement between the physicians;

(2) The provision of controlled substances or dangerous drugs by a physician to a person who the physician has accepted as a patient, if the physician has scheduled or is in the process of scheduling an appointment to examine the patient and the drugs are intended to be used pending that appointment;

(3) The provision of controlled substances or dangerous drugs by emergency medical squad personnel, nurses, or other appropriately trained and licensed individuals,

in accordance with protocols approved by the state board of pharmacy pursuant to rule 4729-5-01 of the Administrative Code; or

(4) The provision of controlled substances or dangerous drugs by a nurse practicing in accordance with a standard care arrangement that meets the requirements of chapter 4723. of the Revised Code and rules promulgated by the board of nursing pursuant thereto.

This paragraph does not authorize or legitimize practices that would violate other applicable standards or legal requirements.

(F) For purposes of this rule, "controlled substance" has the same meaning as in section 3719.01 of the Revised Code.

(G) For purposes of this rule, "dangerous drug" has the same meaning as in section 4729.01 of the Revised Code.

(H) A violation of any provision of this rule, as determined by the board, shall constitute "failure to maintain minimal standards applicable to the selection or administration of drugs," as that clause is used in division (B)(2) of section 4731.22 of the Revised Code; "selling, prescribing, giving away, or administering drugs for other than legal and legitimate therapeutic purposes," as that clause is used in division (B)(3) of section 4731.22 of the Revised Code; and "a departure from, or the failure to conform to, minimal standards of care of similar practitioners under the same or similar circumstances, whether or not actual injury to a patient is established," as that clause is used in division (B)(6) of section 4731.22 of the Revised Code.

Eff. 10/01/99

FOR ADDITIONAL COPIES:

Name: _____

Address: _____

City: _____

State: _____ Zip: _____

Phone: _____

Quantity _____ @ $17.95 per copy: _____

Postage @ $1.00 per copy: _____

TOTAL AMOUNT ENCLOSED: _____

MAKE CHECK PAYABLE TO: FMEW
4856 Sawmill Rd. PMB# 307
Columbus, Ohio 43235